LEARNING AND TEACHING

BY
HAROLD J. SHERIDAN
G. C. WHITE

The University of Chicago
Libraries

Cres Vita
Cat Sci Exco
entia latur

| TRAINING COURSES FOR LEADERSHIP |
| Edited by HENRY H. MEYER and E. B. CHAPPELL |

Learning and Teaching

BY

HAROLD J. SHERIDAN

AND

G. C. WHITE

**Approved by the Committee on Curriculum of the Board of
Sunday Schools of the Methodist Episcopal Church and the
Committee on Curriculum of the General Sunday School
Board of the Methodist Episcopal Church, South**

THE METHODIST BOOK CONCERN
NEW YORK ———— CINCINNATI

———

SMITH & LAMAR
NASHVILLE   DALLAS   RICHMOND

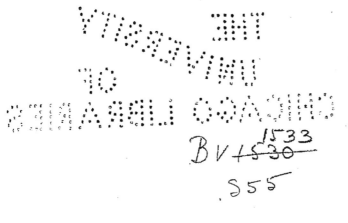

Copyright, 1918
BY
SMITH & LAMAR

570012

LEARNING AND TEACHING

TRAINING COURSES FOR LEADERSHIP

Learning and Teaching. Harold J. Sheridan and G. C. White.

The Training of the Devotional Life. Minnie E. Kennedy and Minna M. Meyer.

The Program of the Christian Religion. John W. Shackford.

The Organization and Administration of the Sunday School. E. M. North and J. L. Cuninggim.

A Methodist Church and Its Work. Worth M. Tippy and Paul B. Kern.

Life in the Making. Wade Crawford Barclay, Arlo A. Brown, Alma S. Sheridan, William J. Thompson, and Harold J. Sheridan.

THE TEACHER'S TASK

TEACHING is not a mechanical but a vital process. It is not simply stuffing the mind of the pupil with information, but presenting truth in such a way as to cause the pupil to receive and appropriate it. "The problem of the teacher is by means of his chosen subject to lead the pupil out into broader fields of thought and to give him an appreciative attitude toward it. It is to bring life and reality into reciprocal relation with the mind of the pupil in such a way that truth may become his personal possession."[1]

Only as truth is received in this vital fashion does it become a means for nourishing the life of the pupil, and to learn how so to present truth as to bring about such a response is an essential part of the teacher's preparation.

Note the use of the word "preparation." We mean to affirm that definite, intelligent preparation is necessary if one would become a real teacher. And this preparation must include a study of methods as well as a study of the subject to be taught. "We sometimes hear," says Professor Weigle, "of 'born teachers.' They are few, and those few love their work too much even to attempt it without preparation. The moment one begins to think of himself as a born teacher he is in danger of losing his birthright."

---

[1] "The Graded Sunday School in Principle and Practice," page 9.

LEARNING AND TEACHING

The purpose of this volume is to help the Sunday school teacher to learn how to teach.

Both of the authors have not only given years of study to the matters which they discuss, but have tested their conclusions by personal experiment and by careful comparison with the methods of the Great Teacher. We recommend them, therefore, as helpful guides. It should be remembered, however, that they are to be regarded by those who study these chapters only as guides. Each student should seek to verify their conclusions or to correct them, if need be, by a first-hand study of boys and girls and by testing the principles laid down in actual practice.

To one who is interested in human life the field of investigation here suggested is one of the most fascinating that modern research has opened up for us. And when to this consideration is added the fact that in the training of childhood and youth we find our greatest opportunity for service, it certainly seems as if young men and women who desire to make their lives count in the development of a real Christian civilization should eagerly avail themselves of the privilege of joining in these studies.   THE EDITORS.

CONTENTS

THE TEACHER'S TASK................................... 5

CHAPTER I
DEVELOPMENT IN THE RELIGIOUS LIFE.................. 9

CHAPTER II
HOW WE LEARN...................................... 17

CHAPTER III
INTERESTS AS THE MOTIVE IN LEARNING................ 27

CHAPTER IV
IMPORTANT FACTORS IN THE LEARNING PROCESS.......... 37

CHAPTER V
DETERMINING VALUES IN MAKING CHOICES.............. 45

CHAPTER VI
THE FORMATION OF HABITS........................... 55

CHAPTER VII
MEMORY 63

CHAPTER VIII
MEETING NEW SITUATIONS............................ 70

CHAPTER IX
LEARNING FROM OUR ASSOCIATES...................... 76

CHAPTER X
THE TEACHER'S TASK AND RESOURCES.................. 83

CHAPTER XI
UNDERSTANDING THE PUPIL A FIRST ESSENTIAL......... 91

LEARNING AND TEACHING

CHAPTER XII

PAGE

THE TEST OF TEACHING MATERIAL...................... 98

CHAPTER XIII

GETTING AND HOLDING THE PUPIL'S ATTENTION.......... 108

CHAPTER XIV

TYPES OF TEACHING.................................. 115

CHAPTER XV

STORY-TELLING...................................... 124

CHAPTER XVI

USING ILLUSTRATIONS 133

CHAPTER XVII

ASKING QUESTIONS 140

CHAPTER XVIII

ACTIVITY IN LEARNING AND LIVING.................... 149

CHAPTER XIX

LEARNING THROUGH DOING............................ 156

CHAPTER XX

THE TEACHER'S LESSON PLANS........................ 166

CHAPTER XXI

TEACHING CHILDREN TO PRAY........................ 177

CHAPTER XXII

THE EMOTIONAL LIFE OF THE LEARNER................. 184

CHAPTER XXIII

THE TEACHER'S FELLOW WORKERS..................... 195

CHAPTER XXIV

EVANGELISM THROUGH TEACHING...................... 202

CHAPTER I

DEVELOPMENT IN THE RELIGIOUS LIFE

A TEACHER of Primary boys and girls had been trying to help her class understand the meaning of Christian service. At the close of the lesson she suggested that each child draw a picture which would tell the story of an act of kindness. When the pictures were finished they were passed around, and each pupil explained what his picture was intended to represent. It was an interesting fact that seven of the eight pictures portrayed the giving of flowers to sick and lonely people. The eighth picture showed a boy loaning his fishing rod to another boy who had no rod of his own. If these illustrations indicated the pupils' appreciation of Jesus's teaching of the meaning of the Christian life, it is evident that they had learned something of the meaning of the words "sick, and ye visited me," but that their idea of Christian service was limited. It would seem that it was not broad enough to include the "naked, and ye clothed me," the "hungry, and ye fed me," and many other things that go to make up the Christian way of living. In a measure, they had comprehended the meaning of service for others, but they had much to learn before they could fulfill the ideal of real Christian living.

Children are not the only ones whose conception of Christian living needs to be broadened. There are many people who sorely need to become much more truly Christian than they now are. There are those who would not think of breaking into a bank

9

LEARNING AND TEACHING

and stealing the money stored there, who would not even pick another person's pocket, but who would be delighted if the street car conductor forgot to collect their fares or if the grocer's clerk omitted to charge all the items of the order delivered. These also need a better knowledge of the Christian way of life.

Especially in the deepest things of religion is growth needed. Many people think of God as merely a little bigger and a little wiser and a little better than themselves. They need to learn that God is a Father in the richest and fullest sense of the word. There are those who say prayers, but who do not really pray. They need to learn the meaning of prayer so well that it will become the highest and dearest privilege of their lives.

The Possibility of Growth

We have evidence, however, not merely that people need to grow, but that they do grow. Jesus took a little company of untrained men and made them statesmen in the work of the kingdom. Little by little he introduced them to the meaning of the new way of life until finally they were ready to take upon themselves the work of the ministry of the gospel. And have we not ourselves seen those who daily grow more like Christ until their lives become so beautiful that they seem to be really living the heavenly life upon the earth? Indeed, have we not in our own lives experienced the joy of progress toward our ideals, of leaving behind our former selves and of pressing "on toward the goal unto the prize of the high calling of God in Christ Jesus"?

DEVELOPMENT IN THE RELIGIOUS LIFE

In the case of children the possibility of growth is even more easily recognized. A small boy known to the writer walked several miles rather than spend five cents to ride on the street car. He felt that he ought to save the money so that he could contribute it to a charitable cause that had been brought to his attention by his teacher. This is but a sample of many incidents indicating progress in Christian character that we witness in the conduct of children. We see the infant who is incapable of moral choice become the sturdy boy or girl with clear convictions of right and wrong. We see the range of the child's moral discrimination increase until finally he is ready for real Christian citizenship. A study of the lives of our pupils will reveal in most cases a steadily increasing sensitivity to moral obligations.

The Laws of Growth

The principle discussed in the preceding paragraphs may seem to be so obvious that there is little need of laying emphasis upon it. It is, however, of such importance to our whole discussion that it can scarcely be overemphasized. If individuals did not need to grow or could not grow in religion, our task as religious educators would be unnecessary and impossible of accomplishment.

There is another fundamental presupposition to our work as teachers—namely, that not only changes in the physical universe, but also developments in human life are not haphazard, but follow definite, intelligible laws. Some of the laws of the universe are very complicated and hard to understand, but little

DEVELOPMENT IN THE RELIGIOUS LIFE

as Jesus gave. A young society girl thought that she was quite deserving of the name Christian because she was giving liberally of her time and money to charitable work, but was apparently unconscious of the fact that in countenancing and defending her father's brewery, which was creating widespread suffering and sorrow, she was acting in a most unchristian manner.

People of all ages need help in understanding what Christianity means. Whatever the age or condition in life, there is still the possibility and need for a better knowledge of the Christian ideal. The boys and girls in our schools need to have many points cleared up. There is the Junior boy who must learn that robbing birds' nests is unchristian. There is the Primary girl who needs to be taught that obeying cheerfully is a Christian virtue. There is the Intermediate who has yet to learn that copying in examinations is unworthy of one of the Master's followers. In spite of all the emphasis that Jesus placed on the Fatherhood of God, many people still hold the early Hebrew idea of God as an exacting judge and a relentless pursuer. Although the prophets in thunderous voices proclaimed the righteousness of God, we still see people going forth to oppress and destroy and carrying as their motto "God with us." The world to-day urgently needs a clearer and a truer knowledge of God.

Feeling and Conduct

An understanding of the teachings of Jesus is of small value unless life is regulated in harmony with them. We must not only see; we must feel and do.

13

LEARNING AND TEACHING

In all walks of life there are many whose deeds do not measure up to the highest that they know. Their knowledge does not grip them so that they are compelled to change their ways of living. When the young woman mentioned above was made to see clearly that both her charity and her luxurious life were made possible by the misery of others and that she was therefore not living as she knew her Master would have her do, she felt deeply remorseful. Her feeling was so strong that she eventually left her father's household and all its comforts to make her own way in the world. The Junior may be told that sorrow comes to the mother bird whose nest is robbed; but unless there is aroused in him real sympathy for the mother bird, he will probably continue to rob birds' nests. As teachers we must learn to make our lessons so vivid and so appealing that the emotions as well as the intellect will be quickened.

There are those who have a great dread of "theology." They seem to think that the student runs the risk of losing his religion. We sometimes hear the same objection to Bible study. Undoubtedly this is in a large measure due to the fact that in some cases feeling does not keep up with knowledge and individuals know better than they do. A better understanding of the Bible and of the ideals of Christian living is certain to be a help to right living, provided that the knowledge is not divorced from feeling and does not paralyze conduct.

Habits of Service

There is another aspect of this matter of growth in the Christian life. Consider, for instance, the

DEVELOPMENT IN THE RELIGIOUS LIFE

individual who believes in foreign missions, who can be stirred by a missionary sermon to the extent of making a generous contribution to the missionary cause, but whose interest in missions lies dormant except when specially stimulated. There is need in this case for the development of a *habit* of missionary interest and effort.

A woman who professed to believe in loving her neighbor as herself lived next door to a needy widow with three small children. When one of the children became very ill, the woman sent flowers every day from her garden to brighten the sick room. When the child recovered, the neighborliness ceased, although the need for it was still urgent.

In a section of one of our cities a number of people are suffering because of unsatisfactory living conditions and insufficient means of support. Occasionally in the spring of the year their suffering is intensified because the river rises and floods the district. At these times their more prosperous fellow citizens are very ready to bring relief, but as soon as the danger from the flood is over their efforts at Christian neighborliness cease. They can be stimulated to acts of Christian service only at times of special crisis.

These are cases where there is need for something more than knowledge and feeling, where the real need is for the development of habits that will lift every day's living toward the ideal of the time of special appeal. One of the important tasks of the teacher of religion is to assist in the formation of these habits of Christian living. The Junior may

15

LEARNING AND TEACHING

easily refrain from robbing birds' nests for a few weeks after the special lesson on the subject. The Primary girl may be glad to help mother care for the baby for a whole week after she hears the story of how Miriam cared for Moses. Our work, however, is not complete until we have made the knowledge and attitudes permanent.

It will be evident how serious is the work which lies before the conscientious teacher. In order to make this work less difficult and more effective it will be necessary for any one who desires to participate in it to make a somewhat detailed study of the laws of growth of the child and of the principles of teaching.

Questions

1. From your own experience mention some cases in which individuals have shown growth in religion.

2. Taking one of the cases that you mentioned in the answer to the question above, point out in just what ways the individual changed.

3. What are the fundamental elements in growth in morals and religion?

4. If religious development were impossible or unnecessary, what difference would that make to our work as teachers of religion?

5. Make a list of some of the questions that you would like to have answered during this course of preparation for Sunday-school teaching.

6. Secure a notebook in which you may record your observation of how pupils actually learn and of how teachers teach. During your study of this book make it a point to use every available opportunity for such observations.

CHAPTER II

HOW WE LEARN

In the last chapter the statement was made that one of the essentials to development in religion is that the pupil should have better conceptions of the meaning of the Christian life. How is the pupil to be taught? What is learning? and what is teaching? Our most commonly used words are at once the hardest to define and the most in need of definition. Certainly it is important that we understand as clearly as possible just what we want to do before attempting to make rules for the doing of it. Some particular cases will help us to be clear regarding the meaning of the two words in question.

Some Typical Cases

What happens when the child in school *learns* the multiplication table? The child who does not know how to multiply gives a wrong answer or hopelessly says, "I don't know," when he sees 2×4 on the board or is asked, "What is three times five?" But let the child learn; and after he has learned he answers promptly eight, or fifteen, whatever the product of the numbers may be. A problem or an arrangement of symbols demanding multiplication calls forth the correct response immediately. Learning in this case is a process of forming definite habits of response to mathematical situations.

Take another example of *learning*. A young man

LEARNING AND TEACHING

enrolls as a student in a dental school. He goes to the clinic and sees patients with decayed teeth. Some are in pain. The health of others is being undermined. All are in need of help. The new student is helpless in the situation. He has through past experience a vague idea that this tooth should be pulled, this cavity be prepared and filled—but he does not know how.

At the end of his course we find the dental student in the clinic again. He is now a skilled dentist. Instead of being nonplused by the situation before him, he feels a steady confidence in his ability to deal with it.

Or consider learning in the case of traits of character. Most of us have to learn self-control. The boy responds to the taunt, the sneer, with angry looks and blows. But later he learns to control his temper. Then his conduct is very different. Discourtesy, even insult, calls forth a laugh, or the soft answer that turneth away wrath, or he turns and walks away. The learning means that he has come to act differently, to respond to the same situation in a new way.

And in the religious life there is learning. Perplexities, sorrows, daily cares are met and dealt with by him who has learned to know God as a constant friend and very present help in trouble in a way very different from that of the man for whom God is a bare intellectual fact.

These illustrations are typical of what is involved in every process of learning. In each case the response made to a certain sort of situation is changed.

18

HOW WE LEARN

Learning is essentially a process of changing the responses to the manifold situations of life—in short, a change from one kind of conduct to another. We say that one has learned well if he has attained to better ways of living. In Christian education the learning process is successful if it results in Christian living on the part of the learner.

The Steps in the Process

Now let us try briefly to analyze the learning process as seen in the illustrations suggested above. In each case we find that the first step in the learning process is realization of the inadequacy of present ways of acting and desire for better ways. The learner is confronted with a situation in which he needs to know how many five times three makes. He can deal with this and similar problems only through knowing the multiplication table. The dental student is spurred to study by the realization that the patient is in need of help that he cannot give. The youth who learns self-control has seen that he does not command respect when he fails to control his temper, or he has come to think of angry quarreling as wrong. Finally, the man who faces sorrow or bears burdens with no solace is, by his sense of need, driven to a search for God.

Whenever an individual sets out to learn a better way of doing something he is driven to his effort by dissatisfaction with present ways of living, a sense of their inadequacy or incompleteness. This dissatisfaction may be manifested as an eager curiosity to know more—that is, dissatisfaction with present

LEARNING AND TEACHHING

knowledge. It may be dissatisfaction with present powers, the desire to do something better or to do more than one can at present. It may be a feeling of inability to cope with a situation that presents itself in the course of normal activities. It may be the consciousness of moral shortcoming or wrong-doing. It may be the sense of the need of something or some one to give unity and harmony, meaning and value to life. In whatever realm, *dissatisfaction with present knowledge is an important preliminary to the improvement of knowledge.*

The next step in learning must be the discovery of new ways of acting. The pupil needs to find out that 2×4 is 8. The dental student needs to find how to use his forceps and his drill, what kind of filling to use, how to place it, and many other things about the whole process of correcting dental troubles. The youth needs to see that it is better to meet trying situations with self-controlled conduct than with an angry temper, and he needs, therefore, to learn how he can best control his temper. The struggling soul must come to realize that fellowship with God will satisfy him in his need.

Economies in Learning

These new ways of responding might be discovered by accident. The animal learns by a process that psychologists call "trial and error." This means that if, for instance, a hungry cat is put in a latched box with food on the outside he will accidentally, after much violent and fruitless activity, hit upon the way to get out. If the process is repeated over and over again, he will, each time with less and less

HOW WE LEARN

effort, rediscover the right movement, and after a large number of trials the right movement will be made immediately. Then the cat is said to have learned. Much human learning partakes of this nature. For example, the acquisition of skill in many athletic sports. But such a learning process is slow and expensive. Fortunately, the human being is not confined to learning of this kind. The dental student of our illustration watches skilled dentists at work and listens to lectures on methods of treatment, and this helps him and saves many mistakes when he tries his own hand. One person can thus learn from the experience of others. He may simply observe another man in his living and working and try to copy him, or he may listen to another's description of his work or his experience in life and profit by it. This profiting by another's experience is an important characteristic of human learning.

These new ways of acting once discovered, the learning process is completed by the *choice* of them and by practice in them until they become "natural" —until there is no hesitation in multiplying, until there is perfection of skill in dentistry, until self-control is easy, until fellowship with God is a part of the daily walk and conversation. These steps we shall consider further in later chapters.

The Teacher's Part

Thus far we have said nothing of teaching and the teacher. What is teaching? and what is the teacher's part in the learning process? *Teaching is simply the exercise of guidance in and control over the*

21

LEARNING AND TEACHING

learning process. It is, then, a process of causing changes in the conduct of others. It is well for the teacher to realize that some sort of learning is inevitable. Between infancy and manhood any individual's ways of living are almost constantly undergoing change. He learns, whether or not he has any teachers in the professional sense. That is why we sometimes speak of nature, of books, of companions as teachers. The teacher in a day school or Sunday school can at best only fit into or have a part in control to a greater or less extent, a process that will go on anyway.

The thought of the teacher as one who guides learning suggests immediately certain requisite qualifications of the teacher who would work well. He is to change ways of living. He must, therefore, know the present lives of his pupils in order that he may be able to estimate wherein change is desirable. He must know, then, how these desirable changes can be produced. This means that he must understand the laws of learning. He cannot change these laws, but he can use them. He can help at each stage of learning. He can help to create the dissatisfaction with present ways of living and the sense of need for better ways in which all learning takes its rise. He can help in the discovery of new and better ways of living by placing at the disposal of the learner his own wider experiences and the experiences of others, by bringing new experiences to his pupil, or by calling his attention to neglected elements of his own experience. Finally, he can furnish opportunities for choice and practice.

HOW WE LEARN

It is the teacher's ultimate purpose to determine ways of living, to influence conduct. He cannot, of course, have conduct constantly under control. His pupils are with him only a fractional part of their lives. He must trust in many cases that right ideas and right feelings will produce right conduct. But a clear realization of the fact that the test of the quality of his work is in the changed lives of his pupils will strengthen him in the determination to use every available means to insure that his teaching shall issue in conduct.

The reader's purpose in studying this course is to obtain assistance in understanding the learning process and hence the teaching process. He is concerned, therefore, first, with the present activities of the learner and the factors that determine them. His primary task, then, is to study the learning process in order to make clear certain general principles or laws that reveal themselves and then to indicate the methods of teaching that conform to these laws of learning and should therefore be most effective.

As teachers we cannot, of course, afford to leave out of account or neglect to formulate the ideal that determines desirable changes in the lives of the learners. On this point, however, only a brief statement lies within the scope of this book. It is our whole conception of Christian living that is determinative of what we shall desire in the lives of our pupils. The teacher's own Christian life and experience will set for him standards by which he estimates his pupils' lives. Our aim as Christian teachers is the bringing of our pupils to Christian

LEARNING AND TEACHING

maturity. This requires that we shall know, appreciate, and make our own the principles and ideals of Christianity; that we shall so understand Christian institutions and methods of work and shall have had such practice in them that we shall be able to participate efficiently in the work of the kingdom; and that we shall know and have practice in the use of the great sources of religious inspiration.

The Great Teacher

Finally, the attention should be turned persistently to the example of the first and greatest of Christian teachers, Jesus. It is well for us to recognize that in only a limited sense is it possible for us to adopt the method of Jesus. We know that his work and teaching were extensive, but our records of his life are very scanty. The author of the fourth Gospel says that if all were written the world would not contain the books. We are really only able to obtain hints as to his teaching methods. We must recognize, further, that our task as teachers is not the same as his task, and in consequence our method of work must be different. He carried on a brief ministry in a circumscribed area, knowing that he must soon leave the work to others. He commissioned his followers to go into all the world and make disciples of all nations. The gradual enlargement of the work involves adaptation and also makes necessary a division of labor and consequent specialization of method.

And may we not be sure that in our work as teachers it is participation in spirit and ideal that we should strive for rather than duplication of

HOW WE LEARN

detail and routine? Christ's call was for fellow workers, not for slavish imitators. His constant emphasis was upon the spirit rather than the letter. We need to try to catch the Christ spirit and the enthusiasm for service that marked his life and then use the gifts bestowed by the Father in the accomplishment of the great tasks of life.

All this is not to say, however, that a study of the methods of Jesus will not help us greatly in our work as teachers. We call him the great Teacher. He faced the hardest aspects of the teacher's work, and he was wonderfully successful. We should, therefore, expect to find illustrated in his work the great principles of our task. We can at least strive to grasp his ideals of the task; to share, with our limitations, his insight into the working of men's minds; and, feeling ourselves colaborers with him, strive to partake of his spirit in our work.

Questions

1. How would you state the aim of Christian education?

2. What would be the test of whether your pupils are learning? Why would not the pupils' knowledge be a satisfactory test?

3. What evidence have you that the Sunday school you know best is really changing the lives of the pupils for the better?

4. What more might be done to make your Sunday school genuinely helpful in influencing life? Consider the question with reference to the Sunday school as a whole, and with reference to particular classes or departments.

5. Considering learning from the standpoint suggested in this chapter, how would you state the function of the curriculum? Of the teacher?

LEARNING AND TEACHING

6. Analyze some particular cases of learning after the plan suggested in the chapter—for instance, the learning of gratitude to God, of obedience, of faith. Might the learning take place in such cases without a teacher? State fully and definitely just what the teacher could do in such cases.

CHAPTER III

INTEREST AS THE MOTIVE IN LEARNING

THE question of motive is an important one for the teacher, because upon the kind of motives that inspire the pupil's activity in learning depends much of the efficiency and permanence of the results. A motive is that which moves, that which causes action. If the pupil is really learning, he is active mentally or physically. And there is some cause for his activity, some motive. The motives that inspire pupils in learning are various. Sometimes it is fear of punishment, a reprimand, a scolding, or severer penalties. Sometimes it is desire for a reward of some kind that has been offered, a place on the honor roll or some more material recognition of "faithful attention to duty." It may be, again, that the pupil wants the favor of the teacher or wishes to make a good showing before the class. He may desire approval or commendation at home, or he may be actuated by the ambition to bring pleasure to parents and friends. Sometimes the work itself is interesting and the activities of learning satisfying in themselves. Children may be taught to read by means of a game in which they place printed placards on objects and persons in the room. The game itself is fascinating and the activity interesting. Again, it may be the pupil realizes that in order to attain some desired end he must perform faithfully certain preliminary tasks. Thus

LEARNING AND TEACHING

a boy learns to read that he may know the story about a certain interesting picture, or when older he devours books about electricity so that he may know how to rig up and use his own wireless outfit. So also the medical student drills himself in technical terms, and the prospective engineer masters the calculus. The effort is necessary for success in the chosen profession.

Kinds of Interest

In each of these cases the motive may be defined as interest in something that seems to the learner desirable or worthy. Interest is the motive in all learning. The processes of learning may be themselves interesting, or the motive may be interest in something to which this learning leads. But *interest of some sort there must be if there is to be any real learning*. The teacher appeals to some sort of interest if he really teaches. Of course if the boy or girl sits in the classroom with his thoughts a thousand miles away or, for that matter, just out of the window or on last week's party or to-morrow's ball game, the teacher is not appealing to any interest. Neither is he teaching. But if the pupil really listens, if he responds as the teacher wishes, if he really learns, it is because of some sort of interest in what is being said or done. The question of motive becomes then a question of choice of interests. What sort of interest should motivate learning?

If we consider the different kinds of motives mentioned above, we see that we may classify them as follows:

INTEREST AS THE MOTIVE IN LEARNING

1. Interest in consequences that have only an artificial relation to the learning activity, interest in punishment to be avoided or in some prize or other reward to be won.

2. Interest in the learning activity itself.

3. Interest in something that seems worth while to the learner and which makes it necessary to learn something else before this desirable thing is possible.

Let us consider each of these kinds of interest in turn.

Fear as a Motive

Here is a pupil who is given a task that he does not understand and that has no meaning for him. He is then forced to do it by threats of penalties to be inflicted for failure. Or he is cowed into keeping quiet and being still by sternness and scoldings.

Is efficient learning possible under such conditions? What really happens here is that the pupil gives just enough attention to his work to enable him to avoid painful results. He is really thinking most intently of the penalty he wants to escape. As a result his attention and activity are divided. His work is not whole-souled. He does one thing half-heartedly while he thinks of something entirely different. There develops a habit of work that is dangerous to mind and character. Disagreeableness comes to be associated with learning in general, and when sooner or later he has the privilege of choosing for himself he chooses to stay away from school. Or instead he becomes an adept in the art of deception, an art which he may carry over into life. Or the definite habit of slovenly, half-hearted work be-

LEARNING AND TEACHING

comes firmly fixed. The principles of good teaching are then opposed to compulsion in the sense of the exercise of superior authority or the use of brute force or the appeal to the motive of fear, except as a last resort and in extreme cases. And even then the teacher should very honestly and candidly ask himself whether the fault may not be with him rather than with the child.

Prizes and Rewards

But there is another danger, quite different and equally to be avoided, to which the Sunday-school teacher is perhaps more liable. While we do not use compulsion, we may choose the way of cajolery, enticement, or bribery. We may not appeal to fear, but we may appeal to the selfish desire for reward or for notoriety or to the love for stimulation and excitement. And these motives are almost as unsatisfactory as the motive of fear.

Against making the desire for pleasant consequences the child's motive precisely similar objections hold as are urged against compulsion. Bribery and "prize-fighting" are as bad as force and the appeal to fear. When the child is offered a prize he works for the prize and not because of his interest in the work itself. "If a boy learns a Bible verse," says Weigle, in "The Pupil and the Teacher," "because he will get a 'ticket' for it, ultimately redeemable in a prize, his interest neither helps him to understand the verse nor begets within him an attitude toward the Bible that is permanently desirable." Interest of a sort is present, but it is not interest in the learning itself nor in anything to which the

INTEREST AS THE MOTIVE IN LEARNING

learning is vitally related. It is external and artificial; so that it means for the child, again, divided attention and divided activity. It leads to instability and selfishness and develops wrong conceptions of the Sunday school and its purposes. To repeat: It is, after all, a question as to what interests shall be used, what motives shall inspire the child. The child acts always from some motive. Some interest is always involved. It is a choice for the teacher between lower and higher. One way is to compel or cajole or entice the pupil—appeal to fear or to the selfish desire for reward or to the love of the pleasurable. There is a better way that is perhaps not so easy. What is this better way?

The Motive of Inherent Interest

This better way is found in using as motives those kinds of interests falling in the second and third groups of our classification. It means searching carefully for those new forms of experience that will appeal to deep and vital interests and consequently meet the real needs of the child's nature. Those activities really influence life that are interesting in themselves or because of their known relationship to some desired end. Only such activities can enlist the learner's whole self, can command undivided attention and sustained and earnest effort. Only such activities are truly educative.

The teacher's task, then, is to fit his material and his methods to the interests of his pupils so as to make these interests serve as motives for learning. The pupil must find the activities of mind and body

LEARNING AND TEACHING

in learning satisfying; he must be conscious of a need, a lack in his own life that only these activities and these truths can satisfy; or he must see this knowledge and this activity as necessary for future achievements in vocation or character. The best work will be done when the pupil wants to work, when the learner wants to learn. And he will want to work only when the work has meaning and interest for him, when he sees its relationships to his own life, when it satisfies the needs of his own nature.

The little child must learn largely by the method of play and from the motive of curiosity. Play and curiosity are two of the fundamental tendencies of his nature. As he grows older various other tendencies appear and cause him to be interested in other things. As these different tendencies manifest themselves at different periods in the lives of our pupils, we should appeal to them as motives for acquiring that knowledge and forming those habits and ideals which go to the making of Christian character and Christian living. *The subject matter and the method of our teaching should have direct relation to the pupil's interests and thus meet his needs at each stage of his development.*

With older pupils we are not, of course, limited to these interests that depend upon the natural tendencies of childhood. The process of learning is constantly building new interests upon these, and the acquired interests may also serve as effective motives in learning. Whatever interest can be appealed to in making the pupil *feel the need* of greater skill, wider knowledge, deeper insight, higher standards,

32

INTEREST AS THE MOTIVE IN LEARNING

better habits, new relationships, and fuller life will be effective as a motive in learning. We need, then, as we have already seen, to know our pupils. And we need this knowledge not only that we may know what in their lives needs changing, but also that we may know what motives we may make effective in bringing about these changes.

Interest in Remote Ends

With our older pupils too we ought, when possible, to appeal to interest in the remote ends to the attainment of which present activities are necessary as means. We must try to show our pupils the relation of the habits we wish them to form, the ideals we wish them to set up, the knowledge we wish them to have, the experiences into which we wish them to enter, to the demands that life will make upon them, life as men, as citizens, and as Christians. We must try to help them hold these things in mind as sufficient motives for earnest endeavor and faithful effort in learning. The ability to control conduct by ideals and by consideration of the future is indispensable to strength of character and efficiency in living.

And, too, by this process of appealing to interest in remote ends we are helping to develop permanently valuable interests. This leads us to the thought of interests as ends or aims in learning. The teacher's aim may be stated in terms of interest. The good man is one who is spontaneously interested in good things, whose interests are worthy. If the teacher has developed in his pupils a genuine and compelling

LEARNING AND TEACHING

interest in worthy things, he has had real success. With such an interest established, whatever may be lacking of needed knowledge will be gained, lines of action will be determined, and choices made in accord with the direction in which the controlling interests lie.

Some Misapprehensions

We may close this chapter by mentioning some misapprehensions that need to be guarded against. In the first place, making interest the motive in learning does not involve looking upon all natural interests as desirable, so that we follow blindly all the child's instinctive tendencies. "Education concerns itself," Strayer writes, "quite as much with the inhibition of undesirable tendencies as with the encouragement of those which lead to desirable activity. The process is not one of following where children lead, but rather of availing ourselves of the native tendencies in order that the ends we desire to achieve may be accomplished with the least waste of time or energy."[1] The native interests of the child are not ends. They are simply means to an end. It is through proper use of them that our purposes for the child are to be accomplished. They are the raw material out of which are to be molded the character and interests that we wish to make the child's permanent possession. Thorndike writes: "The problem is to select for continuance the good and to graft the interest to be acquired upon some interest already present or rather to develop out of some interest already present the one which we seek."

[1] "A Brief Course in the Teaching Process," page 24.

INTEREST AS THE MOTIVE IN LEARNING

Again, making interest the motive does not mean making everything easy for the pupil. It does not mean identifying the interesting with the pleasurable. It does not deny the necessity and the value of effort or hard work; it simply recognizes that a child, like a man, will work best, will work hardest, most efficiently at that in which he is interested because it has some relation to his own life.

In short, appealing to interests in our teaching does not mean allowing the child to "do as he pleases" in the sense of yielding to every random whim of the moment or permitting disorder, insubordination, and laziness. It does not mean that the child shall never do anything "hard." It means simply being reasonable in our teaching by making the child see, to some extent at least, the reason for what he is asked to do. The interest in the pleasurable is not the sole nor the most vital interest of the child. He is interested in many things; and his numerous interests will lead him to activity, to effort, to really hard work, if given a chance. Let the boy really want to do or know something, and no job is too hard for him to tackle, no obstacle big enough to discourage him; he is indefatigable, imaginative, resourceful, constructive. It is simply a matter of the teacher making interests work for him instead of against him.

Questions

1. When do you work most effectively—when you are interested in your work or when it is merely a task to be done?

2. Compare the public schools and the Sunday schools

LEARNING AND TEACHING

as to the possible motives that may be used. **As to the** desirable ones.

3. Can people be driven into the religious life? Can they be enticed into it? Is it desirable that they should be?

4. Consider the Sunday school classes or pupils that you know best. What are the motives in their work? Are these motives commendable? Do they insure learning in the sense of influencing living?

5. What relation would the principles suggested in this chapter and the preceding one have to the planning of the devotional exercises of the Sunday school?

6. What relation would they have to the question of children's attendance upon Church services? Suggest and discuss solutions of this problem.

7. Do the sixteen-year-old boys and girls that you know like Sunday school? Should they? Why? If they do not, what is the trouble? Would making Sunday school interesting by making it seem genuinely worth while and by providing worth-while things to do hold boys and girls in the teen age? Suggest some of these worth-while things.

CHAPTER IV

IMPORTANT FACTORS IN THE LEARNING PROCESS

THE learning process is not complete when right conduct of a given sort is secured once. No teacher of arithmetic would say that a pupil had learned the multiplication table when it has been gone through once. No medical student would feel that he was qualified as an operating surgeon when, under the supervision of the instructor, he had performed one successful operation. The boy has not learned to tell the truth when he has once resisted the temptation to tell a lie. The next time the multiplication table is attempted there may be uncertainty, mistakes, and forgetfulness. The next attempted operation may be bungled by the student of surgery. Next time the boy may take the easiest course and lie. In all learning, doing or saying the right thing once is the first step in the learning process, but it is no more than the first step. The child has not learned the product of 3 × 5 until he always says or thinks 15. The student of medicine has not learned the surgeon's art until he can operate easily and surely. The boy has not learned to tell the truth until he has reached the point where nothing can make him indulge in falsehood. Learning is complete only when tendencies to do and say the right things have been so strengthened and tendencies to do and say the wrong things have been so weakened

37

LEARNING AND TEACHING

that there is no question as to which will determine action. The right things must be done easily and naturally. The tendencies to right conduct must be permanently established in the nature of the learner.

Repetition

How is this result accomplished? We find the answer easily if we consider some cases in which it is accomplished. Watch the boy who wants to play baseball well. He takes the field and spends the whole afternoon catching flies batted to him by another boy. The next afternoon he is out again going through the same performance. He throws to the bases over and over again. He takes his turn hitting at thrown balls, one after another. Again and again he bats and catches and throws, all the time with no thought for anything except doing those particular things well. His "whole soul" is in his ball-playing.

Or consider the recruit in the army. Hours each day are given, with undivided attention, to responding to this command and that, over and over again, until the responses become automatic. Not until they do is learning complete.

These illustrations suggest to us that *repetition is an important factor in learning.* And we notice, too, that it is repetition with *attention* that is effective. The ambitious ball player cannot afford to practice with his thoughts elsewhere. Nor can the soldier afford to give less than his undivided attention to his work.

The maxim "Practice makes perfect" is very generally recognized. Susanna Wesley is said to have

IMPORTANT FACTORS IN PROCESS

replied when asked why she told her sons the same thing twenty times: "Because nineteen is not enough." We find Jesus using not one parable, but many, to show his disciples the nature of the kingdom he had come to establish. His "Verily, verily" was a means of attracting attention and making his teaching impressive. From the simplest to the highest forms of learning, repetition is essential. It is through repetition that the multiplication table and correct spelling and pronunciation and the meaning of words in a foreign vocabulary are learned. The prospective physician must diagnose many cases and perform many operations under the critical direction of instructors before he is skilled as a healer of disease. The law student argues many cases in "moot court" or classroom before he can be admitted to the bar. The prospective teacher works in the practice school under competent supervision before being intrusted with the care of a class of her own. Learning in all these cases involves constant practice.

And it is through practice, too, that habits of thoughtfulness and kindness and cheerfulness and trustfulness in relation to one's fellows and gratitude and reverence and love toward God become attitudes that determine daily living. One unselfish act does not make an unselfish character. The unselfish character means a character in which the habit of unselfishness is established. And such habits can be established only by the persistent repetition of unselfish acts. The loftiest trait of Christian character, one which embraces all the virtues, god-

39

LEARNING AND TEACHING

liness, or godlikeness, can be the product only of persistent fellowship with God. "The practice of the presence of God" is the suggestive phrase chosen as the title for the published meditations of one of the medieval saints. All the acquired traits of intellect, character, and skill involve in their acquisition this principle of repetition, of exercise, of practice.

Punishments and Rewards

A consideration of some other cases of learning will indicate to us a second important factor in learning. Watch an animal trainer. When the horse he is trying to teach a new trick does the right thing, he is rewarded with a lump of sugar. When he does the wrong thing, he is punished with the whip. Why? Because the trainer knows that the reward will act as an incentive, the punishment as a deterrent. As a result the horse will be more likely to do the right thing and less likely to do the wrong thing next time. If we turn to human learning, we find the same principle at work. A baby girl just beginning to walk got a fall on the hard pavement. For weeks she made no further attempt to walk alone. But on a visit to the country she was encouraged to try again on the soft grass. The successful attempt was rewarded by praise and further encouragement, and as a result she learned to walk easily. The discomfort of a fall deterred her; the satisfaction of success and praise encouraged her. The boy on the baseball field by pitching a certain kind of curve ball has the satisfaction of striking out the opposing batter. That is the kind

IMPORTANT FACTORS IN PROCESS

of curve that he will throw later rather than one that has been hit for a home run. The lawyer impresses the jury and wins his case by a particular style of oratory. The satisfaction of success causes him to adopt that style next time rather than a style that has failed to achieve success for him. The pupil in school answers a question correctly. He wins the approval of his teacher and the admiration of his mates. The resulting satisfaction makes a little surer his knowledge of that answer. The Sunday-school pupil overcomes a temptation and knows the satisfaction of moral victory. And he is that much stronger for the next fight. The Christian under trial seeks strength in prayer. The peace that comes to him is a guarantee that prayer will be a larger factor in his life than heretofore.

The Law of Effect

All these instances illustrate a second important principle in learning, the "law of effect." The law of effect is that if a certain response to a situation produces satisfaction that response is more likely to be made in the future and that, on the other hand, discomfort resulting from a response decreases the chances of that response being made subsequently. Briefly, "satisfying results strengthen, and discomfort weakens the bond between situation and response." This has been called "one of the greatest, if not the greatest, laws of human life. Whatever gives satisfaction, that mankind continues to do. We learn only that which results in some kind of satisfaction. Because of the working of this law

LEARNING AND TEACHING

animals learn to do their tricks, the baby learns to talk, the child learns to tell the truth, the adult learns to work with the fourth dimension." "It is the great weapon of all who wish—in industry, trade, government, religion, or education—to change men's responses, either by reënforcing old and adding new ones or by getting rid of those that are undesirable."

But we may well raise the question, What is the nature of this satisfaction that is so important a factor in "stamping in" right responses? Evidently we do not mean mere physical pleasure or freedom from pain. Freedom from threatened pain, assured physical well-being may frequently be an effective form of this satisfaction, it is true. The boy who escapes punishment by performing his task enjoys a very genuine satisfaction. So, too, the boy who has been rewarded by a prize. But there are forms of satisfaction that do not come as natural consequences of the responses themselves; the connection is artificial. There are higher and more effective forms of satisfaction. First, there may be the satisfaction that comes from the exercise of some instinctive tendency. Play is in itself satisfying to the child; finding out things is satisfying to his curiosity; building houses and modeling are satisfying to his constructive instincts; because of an instinctive urge he finds satisfaction in making collections. The teacher who can enlist some natural tendency of his pupils in whole-hearted activity will be assured of satisfaction resulting from the activity itself. The desire for the approval of others has an instinctive

IMPORTANT FACTORS IN PROCESS

basis; and the satisfaction that comes from having won such approval from parents, from teachers, and from playmates is frequently an effective and not unworthy form of satisfaction if it is not allowed to become selfish or conceited or gloating.

The Highest Forms of Satisfaction

But undoubtedly the highest form of satisfaction is that that comes from the sense of a need met, a problem solved, a difficulty overcome, a felt lack in one's life supplied. The boy who wants to make a rabbit trap or a kite will spend hours of earnest effort in discovering how, and the satisfaction that comes to him in his success is deeper and more genuine than any artificial reward could possibly give. Let your pupils feel a genuine need for the knowledge that they know you can give them. Let them have an active interest in finding the answers to questions, the solutions to problems, the meaning of words, or the most helpful ways in which they can be of service to others, and the satisfaction that will result from their efforts will insure as nothing else can the retention of those particular forms of activity as permanent elements in their lives. And in the higher stages of learning we may have that finest form of satisfaction that comes from a sense of duty done, of ideals realized, of principles maintained, of spiritual promptings and yearnings satisfied.

Motive

Obviously this law of effect is closely related to the question of motive. What shall be the pupil's motive in learning? The pupil's motive is the antic-

LEARNING AND TEACHING

ipation of the satisfaction that will result. This question of motive we have already discussed in Chapter III. As was made clear there, since the satisfyingness of the response is so important, as teachers we must see to it that the right responses are genuinely satisfying to our pupils in anticipation as well as in realization. And the most effective form of satisfyingness is that which is the natural outcome of the activity itself. So, too, the most effective form of discomfort is that which the child understands to be a natural consequence of his actions. The child who sees that his misbehavior makes it necessary that he be put out of the room so that he shall not interfere with the work of others is being much more effectively disciplined from the educational standpoint than the child who is whipped or scolded or kept in after school.

These two, the law of exercise and the law of effect, are fundamental laws of learning. Along with certain supplementary principles, they are operative in the development of skill, in the acquisition of knowledge, in the formation of moral or intellectual habits, in the organization of living around ideals and general principles. In later chapters we shall try to see their operation in certain particular forms of learning.

Questions

1. Of what value is repetition in the learning process?

2. Mention some cases, other than those referred to in the chapter, where repetition is necessary to real learning.

3. Show how satisfaction plays a part in the learning process.

4. What is the difference between prizes and other artificial rewards, and what are called natural rewards?

44

CHAPTER V

DETERMINING VALUES AND MAKING CHOICES

As Christian teachers we are concerned primarily with the moral and religious lives of our pupils. Now, religion and morality cannot be forced upon any one nor inculcated by any mechanical process. The animal is capable of being trained. But we never speak of an animal's behavior as moral or immoral. However far the process of animal training may be carried, there is always lacking an element essential to morality in even its simplest forms. The animal's behavior cannot be called moral. Why? Because nowhere in the process of training does the animal exercise choice as we understand it. His responses are throughout mechanically determined. He is governed wholly by present stimuli. He does not foresee consequences and consciously apply his past experience to the present situation. He is not responsible. And the essence of morality is responsibility expressed in choice. So we do not hold the insane person who steals or kills responsible, because he lacks the power of rational choice, of controlling his own conduct in accordance with ideas and ideals. And we consider the child capable of moral or immoral conduct only when and in so far as he is able to choose for himself between this or that line of action because of his discernment of right and wrong.

45

LEARNING AND TEACHING

Moral Conduct

For conduct to have moral quality it must be voluntary. Moral conduct depends upon the choice of the individual. It involves the weighing of values, the consideration of alternative lines of action, and the selection of one of them in preference to the others. It necessitates deliberation, thinking. If we choose for our pupils and force or coerce them into conforming to our choice, we must not cherish the hope that in so doing we are developing in them moral character. We may be establishing good habits. The securing of right responses by any means may be useful in that such responses may later be chosen by the individual and held in his life, because he recognizes their value and identifies them with his ideals. But no habit is moral in the true sense unless it be built upon past choices of that kind of conduct by the individual acting as a self-guiding agent. And habits otherwise established become an element in the moral character only when they have been definitely chosen for retention by the individual possessing them. We must see to it that habits formed, whether through individual choice or otherwise, are desirable. Habits of honesty, obedience, reverence, thoughtfulness of others early established in the child's life may later through his personal choice become effective elements in character. To allow the child to get into the grip of bad habits because we think him unable to understand and choose for himself is, of course, folly. But the point to be urged here is that we must not be content with the mere mechanical formation of even good habits.

DETERMINING VALUES

As soon as possible, and wherever possible, we must see to it that our pupils choose for themselves desirable modes of conduct because they see their value. It is thus only that they can develop real character expressed in habits built upon these choices and in ideals which govern conduct in times of crisis when further choice is necessary.

The Basis of Choice

Changing the conduct of our pupils is not enough. We must see to it that the changes occur because the pupils want them to occur, that the better ways of living are adopted because they themselves choose them in preference to others.

Jesus in his life on earth was continually changing men's lives. He is still doing so. And he is securing, not an enforced adoption of his program, but the most willing and determined adherence to his plans. How is it accomplished?

Let us examine an instance of a life changed through Jesus's influence. Zaccheus was a publican who had grown rich in his despised business. He had evidently heard a great deal about Jesus, and when Jesus came to Jericho Zaccheus made up his mind to see him. But he realized that he "could not see for the crowd, because he was little of stature." So he ran on ahead and climbed up into a sycamore tree in order that he might get a good view. What was his motive? Largely curiosity, doubtless. He was willing to endure the inconvenience and discomfort of the position in order to satisfy that curiosity.

LEARNING AND TEACHING

Now, Jesus came and called him to "make haste and come down." And Zaccheus "made haste and came down and received him joyfully." Why? Because Jesus told him to do so. But mere telling is not always enough. If securing right conduct were merely a matter of advising people, it would be a much simpler task than it is. Zaccheus came down because he felt that by coming down he would have something far more worth while than a fine view. The change in his conduct was due to the arrival of new facts, the knowledge of Jesus's attitude toward him.

A little later we find Zaccheus changing the whole plan of his life. Before his experience with Jesus money seems to have been his chief desire. But now he has a new scale of values. Justice and righteousness are worth more than gold, and he is willing to make fourfold restitution for the wrongs he has done.

A like case is that of Matthew. Jesus came and called him. Matthew's work had been profitable to him. Upon it depended his livelihood. But here are greater values to be realized, beside which mere pecuniary gain counts as nothing. "And he arose and followed him." With the rich young ruler, whom Jesus loved, the trouble was that his scale of values was wrong. He desired eternal life. No flaw could be found in his conformity to the law. But he could not sacrifice the less for the greater. He went away sorrowful, but nevertheless he went away.

Here, then, is the principle. *The pupil will change*

48

DETERMINING VALUES

his conduct if he feels that the proposed plan will bring him greater worth than the present plan.

The Choice of the Less Valuable

Now let us examine a case that at first may seem to be a contradiction to this. What about the individual who habitually indulges in alcohol? He resolves never to drink again. He signs the pledge. So far he is illustrating the principle perfectly. He drank because he expected enjoyment therefrom. Now he sees his family in need; he sees himself out of work; he realizes that he is socially ostracized; he probably suffers physical discomfort from the after effects of the drug. He *feels* that in the future temperance will be much more desirable. He resolves to abstain. Now comes the crisis. Soon afterwards, sorely tempted, he yields. What happened to change his conduct from the plan he had in mind when he signed the pledge? The difference lies here: that, whereas he made his resolution when not in temptation, he yielded when the appetite was very severe. At the one time he felt keenly that temperance was really worth while. At the other time he still remembered, at least in part, the values to be gained by abstinence, but he suffered so intensely from the need that he concluded that the gain was not worth the price.

The Importance of Feeling

We must, then, cause our students actually to *feel* that certain lines of conduct will bring more satisfactory results than others. It is, therefore, not hard to see why some of our teaching is not person-

LEARNING AND TEACHING

ally appropriated by the learner. It is because he does not see the significance of the points we are trying to make. As a lesson in obedience we tell a six-year-old child a story of how a soldier always obeyed his officers and was therefore promoted to be an officer. The next day the child is told to come away from the window and sit on a chair near the radiator. Here is an opportunity for him to practice his lesson in soldierlike obedience. Think of what goes on in his mind. He thinks that by staying by the window he will be able to see the interesting things outside. If he sits on the chair, he will miss that and will have nothing to do. If he stays at the window, he will incur his parents' displeasure. The factors in the case are interesting things to be seen outside plus displeasure of parents *versus* a dull time on the chair plus parents' approval. He weighs it up and decides. If the displeasure is really to be feared, he probably obeys. If he is not much afraid, he disobeys. In any case he acts in the way that he feels will bring him the greatest satisfaction. The soldier, so far as he can see, has nothing to do with the case. A story of a boy who sat by the window and caught a severe cold might have had an effect.

Here, again, is a little fellow who is tempted to lie. The lie would enable him to escape rebuke or punishment. This seems desirable to him. If that consideration alone enters into his thoughts, the lie will be told. But he knows that his telling a lie would pain his mother. He loves his mother, and to give her pain pains him. This is to his mind a higher consideration. But perhaps he may think

50

DETERMINING VALUES

mother will never know. Then still higher values must enter in if the victory is to be won for honesty. He knows that lying is wrong; and doing wrong is displeasing to God, who loves him and whom he loves. Just so, whatever the issue, conduct is determined in accordance with the scale of values that has been established.

In our work, then, as teachers we must put the pupil in possession of the data that will enable him to decide values wisely. He must not only know the facts, but must *feel* their significance. This can be felt only if he can see their relation to his own life.

The Value of Clear Thinking

Moreover, we must emphasize the importance of stopping to think and must furnish opportunities where the learner is encouraged to choose for himself, to stop and analyze the situation that confronts him, to act only after deliberation, anticipation of consequences, weighing of values. Thinking occurs in situations where an actual problem is confronted, alternative lines of action are possible, and choice is necessary. Such problems arising in the pupil's experience are the best possible training in moral thoughtfulness. Thoughtfulness, together with moral sensitiveness and genuine responsiveness to moral values, constitutes the virtue of conscientiousness, which is indispensable in Christian living. This sensitiveness to moral values and this willingness to stop and think before acting are traits to be cultivated. At the close of Chapter IV. we suggested that there are certain supplementary principles op-

LEARNING AND TEACHING

erative along with the laws of repetition and effect. One of these principles is that one aspect or element of a situation may determine our conduct with reference to that situation. The significance of this law for the moral life is found in the fact that the same situation may call forth quite different responses, moral or immoral, according as one or the other element in it attracts attention or is uppermost in consciousness. This is made clear in the instances already studied. Zaccheus, Matthew, the truthful boy, acted rightly by holding their attention upon the higher values. The rich young ruler and the drunkard failed because of the power of the less worthy considerations. Let us examine a further case.

Thoughtfulness

A group of boys wish to celebrate an athletic victory of their school. The idea occurs to them to make a bonfire of a neighbor's fence. Let them think only of the victory to be celebrated, the fun and excitement of the fire, and the fence will be burned. But let them be reminded that the rights of another person are involved; that trespassing on his rights will cause him annoyance and inconvenience and loss; that the act will mean not simply a good time, but doing wrong; and if the reminder is strong enough or right impulses in connection with such considerations have been sufficiently established, the material for the fire will be sought elsewhere. The boys' response to the same total situation will thus be quite different, according as one or another element in it is held in the mind and so determines

DETERMINING VALUES

action. Much boyish wrongdoing, and adult wrong-doing too, is due, not to evil impulses, but to sheer thoughtlessness or ignorance, failure to see a situation in the right way, neglect of certain aspects of it.

It is important, then, that we train our pupils to stop and think, to analyze situations. We must make them realize that thoughtlessness is so poor an excuse as to be no excuse at all. If the boy can see clearly and remember that his fellow's shabby clothes represent self-denial and suffering on the part of his poor parents, he will take a different attitude from the one he takes when he remembers only that they look funny. The boy at college who can get his thoughts centered on dishonesty or stealing as an element in the temptation to "crib" on examinations, instead of thinking exclusively of the pass or the higher grade, will be much less likely to cheat. Calling things by their right names is an important influence in moral conduct. Understanding and remembering what is really involved means neglecting no aspect of a situation and letting the right aspect determine one's response.

The Value of Practice

Finally, we must not only provide the data, see to it that values are felt, and provide opportunities for making choices. We must, in addition, make sure, in so far as we can, that the choices issue in action. However correct one's ideas or however lofty one's ideals, they must express themselves in action, they must influence living, if they are to be worth anything. Conduct is the test of character.

LEARNING AND TEACHING

The morality of the pupil must be progressive. Growth in the moral and religious life means that as experience widens and deepens conduct comes more and more under the control of the more worthy values, the values that are lofty and permanent. In the unfolding life there must be a constant "revaluation of values" until finally there is attained the fullness of the stature of the perfect man in Christ Jesus, for whom the supreme value is the consciousness of acceptance with God and of God's approval on every word and deed.

Questions

1. What is the difference between moral and nonmoral conduct?

2. Just what is it that leads to choice?

3. Why do people sometimes choose the less valuable?

4. What part has clear thinking in the attainment of moral character?

CHAPTER VI

THE FORMATION OF HABITS

AFTER values are determined and choices made, the desirable modes of activity must become permanent elements in the life of the learner. They may become permanent elements either (1) as habits, (2) as remembered facts, or (3) as ideals and general principles around which the life is organized and in the light of which later choices are made. In this chapter we shall consider the formation of habits.

The Meaning of Habit

Habitual action is action that is performed automatically, independently of conscious guidance, as a result of training or experience. It is thus marked off from instinctive action by the fact that it depends upon previous experience. It is acquired, learned; while instincts are inherited, inborn. It is distinguished from voluntary action by its independence of conscious guidance.

One can very easily convince himself of the importance of habit if he will simply observe his behavior throughout a single day and endeavor to classify his actions as instinctive, habitual, or voluntary. Try this. You may be surprised to note how large a part of your daily life is gone through in purely automatic fashion and how infrequently "will power" has to be exercised. William James estimates that "ninety-nine hundredths or possibly nine hundred and nine-

LEARNING AND TEACHING

ty-nine thousandths of our activity is purely automatic and habitual."

In a sense all learning is a process of habit formation, and all our mental life depends upon the laws of habit. The laws of habit formation, then, will be in no way different from the laws of learning in general. We speak of intellectual habits. Memorizing a passage is really a process of making habitual the connections between one word and another or between one idea and another. The laws of association that lie at the basis of all our mental life are the laws of habit applied to ideas. Habits of action depend upon connections formed between situations and responses. Memory, imagination, and reasoning depend upon connections formed between one idea and another. The processes are at bottom one. We find Rousseau saying: "Education is nought but the formation of habits."

Usually, however, we give more specific meaning to the term "habit." The point to note carefully here is that habit formation is but a specific application of the laws of learning already outlined. Habits are formed when the connections between situation and response are made automatic through repetition. In speaking of a person's habits we usually have in mind either his customary direct responses to the various situations that life presents or such moral traits of his life as temperance, generosity, unselfishness, and the like. These moral habits are organized groups of responses. Walking is a habit. Taking a certain route from the home to the office or to school day after day is a matter of habit. Using

56

THE FORMATION OF HABITS

knives and forks and spoons, buttoning and unbuttoning our collars, tying our ties, lacing our shoes— these are habits. Rising at six-thirty, whatever the allurements of an extra quarter of an hour in bed, may be made a matter of habit. Smoking is a habit. Writing with pen or typewriter is a matter of habit. Daily exercise is a habit. Examples might be multiplied indefinitely up to the "habit of attention," the habit of self-sacrifice, the habit of abstinence, the habit of prayer—all the habits that characterize the good man or the contrary habits that characterize his immoral neighbor.

Good and Bad Habits

Shall the habits of our pupils be good or bad? The Sunday-school teacher has his pupils only a very small part of their time. He really gets very little chance at them, and his opportunity to help in determining their habits may seem very limited. Half an hour on the streets every day during the week may so easily undo what he has tried to do in that brief period on Sunday. But the teacher can comfort himself with the thought that other agencies are at work with him for the good of the pupil—the home, the day school—in all save the exceptional cases. And the Sunday-school teacher needs to understand how he can help, so that he may use to best advantage such opportunity as he has, and so that, further, he may be able, when opportunity offers, to instruct his pupils in the best ways of building good habits and overcoming bad ones for themselves.

LEARNING AND TEACHING

The Building of Habits

The principles of habit formation may be very simply stated: (1) Get a good start; (2) repeat the desired actions until they have become automatic; (3) permit no exceptions to occur until the process is complete.

The first point takes us back to the question of motive. The stronger the pupil's motive for the formation of the new habits, the deeper and more genuine his interest in acquiring them, the easier and surer his success. This is what James means by his advice: "In the acquisition of a new habit, or the leaving off of an old one, we must take care to launch ourselves with as strong and decided an initiative as possible." He continues in words that are clear and to the point and of particular value to the teacher, one of whose chief interests is in the moral lives of his pupils: "Accumulate all the possible circumstances which shall reënforce the right motives; put yourself assiduously in conditions that encourage the new way; make engagements incompatible with the old; take a public pledge, if the case allows; in short, envelop your resolution with every aid you know. This will give your new beginning such a momentum that the temptation to break down will not occur as soon as it otherwise might; and every day during which a breakdown is postponed adds to the chance of its not occurring at all." Thorndike has called this principle the "law of impetus" and has stated it briefly: "Make the new connection with full energy and zeal." Still more

THE FORMATION OF HABITS

simply we may say as suggested above, "Get a good start."

After getting a good start, persistence is the essential thing in the establishment of the new habit. The "law of repetition" Thorndike has summed up in the words: "Give the habit exercise." To be most effective, however, it is important to note, the repetition must be attentive repetition. The value of this attention in repetition is most apparent in memory drill and in the acquisition of skill of one sort or another—in learning to write, for example, or to draw. But the principle has general application. The activities in which the pupil engages that do not interest him and therefore fail to hold his undivided attention, activities into which he does not put his whole self, will never become habitual. Dropping a nickel every Sunday into the collection box will never develop the habit of cheerful giving unless the teacher adopts some method of helping the pupils to understand why they give and gets them interested in giving.

On the third factor we may quote James again. "Never suffer an exception to occur until the new habit is securely rooted in your life. Each lapse is like the letting fall of a ball of string which one is carefully winding up; a single slip undoes more than a great many turns will wind again. . . . It is necessary, above all things, . . . never to lose a battle. Every gain on the wrong side undoes the effect of many conquests on the right."[1] This is called the "law of constancy."

---

[1]"Psychology," pages 145, 146.

LEARNING AND TEACHING

To these principles James adds another suggestion: "Seize the very first possible opportunity to act on every resolution you make and on every emotional prompting you may experience in the direction of the habits you aspire to gain. . . . No matter how full a reservoir of maxims one may possess, and no matter how good one's sentiments may be, if one has not taken advantage of every concrete opportunity to act, one's character may remain entirely unaffected for the better."[1]

Not only is it important for the teacher to be familiar with the principles of habit formation in order that he may follow them in his work; it is highly desirable that the pupil himself should be instructed in them so that he himself may apply them in his efforts to build good habits or break bad ones. To know the value of a good start, the danger of permitting a single exception, the necessity for acting and of making opportunities for acting in accord with one's resolution should be helpful to every pupil in whom has been aroused a real aspiration to control and direct his life rationally and efficiently.

The Limitations of Habit

Before leaving the question of habit this ought to be said: Habit has its limitations. We do not wish our pupils to become slaves of habit, even though the habits are good ones. The person who is to live efficiently must have the power of remaking his habits when they prove inadequate. Conditions change, new problems confront any one who keeps alive, and

---

[1]"Psychology," pages 146, 147.

THE FORMATION OF HABITS

the person is pitiable who lacks the power to adjust himself to changed circumstances, to face new problems, who stands dazed and helpless because he has no habit to fall back upon, no customary way of acting that is adequate, however adequate his equipment of habits may have been for the routine affairs of his life or for familiar situations. And a Church made up of such individuals will fall behind and fail to adapt itself to changing conditions and so be unable to meet ever new and more complex demands made upon it by an increasingly complex civilization and social order. Sometimes a youth goes out from a good home with its Christian influence and careful training in habits of right conduct and, in the new conditions of college or the business world, goes to pieces. He had not been trained to stand alone and confront perplexities and problems. This desirable trait has been called "the habit of rehabituating one's self."

And this is not simply a matter of acquiring new virtues. Each standard of life and conduct must be capable of application to new situations as well as to old and familiar ones. The sense of justice that is sensitive to the wrongs of the man who has property stolen from him, but that is insensible to the evils of child labor or industrial oppression—products of a new social order—such a sense of justice is an unreliable guide to Christian living.

Our pupils and the Church need to be guarded against rigidity and woodenness of character. Good habits need to be allied in the fully rounded character with enlightened judgment, the willingness and

LEARNING AND TEACHING

the ability to remake one's habits, to strike out on new lines when occasion demands. An important part of learning is acquiring the ability to form new habits for one's self when they are needed. This necessitates the setting up of *conscious* guides to right conduct and the formulation of general principles and standards and ideals that may govern when fixed habits prove inadequate for changing conditions. We shall wish to consider this phase of learning in a later chapter.

Questions

1. Just what is the difference between acts that are controlled by habit and those that are not so controlled?

2. What are the steps in habit formation?

3. How would you set out to establish in your pupils the habit of Church attendance? Of daily prayer and Bible reading?

4. How would you proceed to break up an undesirable habit?

5. When do habits become a hindrance rather than a help?

CHAPTER VII

MEMORY

THE ability of our pupils to use the wider experience that we give them in the form of facts and information depends in a large measure upon their memory of them. This means at least two things: (1) The information must be retained, and (2) when needed it must be subject to call. All our teaching that aims at supplying information, at increasing the knowledge of our pupils, then, involves memorizing on their part. When we think of memory in this broad sense, it is evident that all that was said in Chapter IV. relates directly to memory. As of habit, so of memory it may be said that it is but a specific application of the general laws of learning. As habit involves making connections between situation and action, memory involves the establishing of connections between facts and ideas, so that one fact or idea is responded to with another fact or idea. The effectiveness of memory thus depends, so far as we can control it, upon the care with which the proper method is followed in learning.

The Dependence of Memory on Learning

A good memory depends upon proper learning. We may say, then: (1) That will be best remembered which is best understood and which has most meaning, significance, interest, relation to the pupil's own life at the time when he first becomes ac-

63

LEARNING AND TEACHING

quainted with it. The discussions of interest as the motive in learning, of apperception, and of the rôle of satisfaction, in earlier chapters have emphasized this point. (2) That will be best remembered which is brought into relation with other facts and principles, which becomes a part of the organized system of ideas. We shall wish to discuss this organization of living more fully in a later chapter. James says: "Of two men with the same outward experiences, the one who thinks over his experiences most and weaves them into the most systematic relations with each other will be the one with the best memory." (3) That will be best remembered that has been expressed in action. This point also is to be developed in a later chapter. The boy who applies the Golden Rule is the boy who will remember it best.

In other words, in this broad sense, helping the pupil to memorize is a matter of (1) enlisting the pupil's interests and relating the new experiences to those he already has, so that attention is secured and the new experiences understood; (2) helping him to think, or to organize his knowledge and to put it into a system; (3) getting him to act upon his knowledge, to express it in conduct. In brief, it is a matter of teaching well.

Sometimes we limit the meaning of "memorizing" and use it to signify "learning by heart," committing things to memory word for word. What of memory in this sense? Two questions suggest themselves with reference to this sort of memory work:

MEMORY

"What?" and "How?" We may best answer the question "What?" by first asking "Why?"

The Value of Memory

Why do we wish our pupils to learn some things "by heart"? In the secular school they must learn the alphabet and the multiplication table and the sums and differences of numbers. These things will be indispensable in the acquisition of further knowledge. They are useful. There would be no particular value in learning them apart from their practical usefulness. So, too, in the Sunday school some things need to be learned because they are useful in just this way: they make possible further learning. Again, in the secular school the pupil is required to commit to memory some of the great passages of literature, Lanier's "Marshes of Glynn," Portia's speech on mercy, Lincoln's Gettysburg address. Why? If the material has been well chosen, the passages will enter into and influence the life of the pupil in valuable ways, will help him to clearer expression, furnish him with noble ideas, inspire him to better living. For such purposes as these the Sunday school can supply material for "committing to memory" that nothing in the secular literature of the world can equal.

Usefulness, then, is the sole justification for the requirement that a thing shall be memorized word for word, usefulness in the sense of making easier further learning or in the sense of value in influencing thought and conduct. To this test of usefulness our memory material should be brought in an-

LEARNING AND TEACHING

swering the question, "What?" Fortunately, the individual teacher does not have to answer this question wholly for himself. Suggestions as to memory material are made in the textbooks and other lesson helps. But it is well for the teacher to have a basis for judging the suggestions and determining their wisdom with reference to his pupils and their individual capacities.

Certainly every Bible student should know the number, the names, and the order of the books of the Bible. Some geographical knowledge concerning Palestine is essential. These are illustrations of the kind of knowledge that is valuable, not in itself, but because it facilitates the gaining of further knowledge. As to the second sort of knowledge, specific suggestions in any detail are not needed here. Certainly the Ten Commandments, the Lord's Prayer, the twenty-third Psalm, the Beatitudes would occur at once to any one. Some of the great hymns of the Church should by all means be included.

The Right Time for Memorizing

But when we have selected all the material that we think worth memorizing by our pupils, we need to answer another question: "When?" For there is another test to which our memory material should be subjected: the test of meaningfulness for the pupil. Understanding is the first step in memorizing. Only when they understand it, when it has meaning for them and finds a place in their own lives in relation to their own experiences, does a passage "learned by heart" really have any value to a pupil.

66

MEMORY

We sometimes require a pupil to commit a passage to memory because we think it will have meaning and value for him "some day." But this is a dangerous practice. In the first place, we have evidently failed to influence the child's life *now*, and thus we have missed an opportunity. Such knowledge has been compared to a stone placed between the branches of a tree, which may in the end be surrounded and covered by the trunk; or to a bullet lodged in the human body. The stone never becomes a part of the tree, nor the bullet of the body. So this meaningless material "learned by heart" never becomes a part of the mental and spiritual life. And more than this, we run the risk, every time we compel the memorizing too soon of one of the great passages, of establishing a distaste for that passage and perhaps for the Bible itself that may never be wholly overcome. We need, then, to be careful not to compel our pupils to memorize material that is wholly meaningless and distasteful, justifying ourselves on the ground that at some time in the future it will take on meaning or in the mistaken notion that we are thereby "improving the memory."

This does not involve failure to recognize the fact that any great passage takes on new and deeper and richer meaning as experience broadens and deepens. We cannot demand that our pupils understand fully and completely. There is much of Scripture that no one understands in its fullness as yet. But we can require that what they learn by heart shall have real meaning to our pupils, that they shall understand in part, and that their understanding shall

LEARNING AND TEACHING

not be a misunderstanding which will mislead and will have to be corrected later.

As to "improving the memory," psychology tells us that the power to retain can be very little, if at all, modified; that our "retentive capacity" is dependent upon the quality of the tissue of the nervous system; that that is fixed at birth; and that no amount of practice can have much effect upon it. The memory can be improved, but the best way to improve the memory is to improve the methods of learning.

How to Memorize

This brings us to the question of "How?" The first step in effective memorizing, as has already been suggested, is understanding; and the teacher's first task is to help his pupil in understanding the passage to be learned. This understanding is more than the first step. For by going over and over a passage in the effort to get its meaning, to appreciate the thought, to see its relation to his life, the pupil has taken a long step in the direction of memorizing it. Understanding it in this thorough sense, all that is necessary in order to insure its permanent retention is *repetition*—saying it over and over again, not in a purely mechanical way, but with attention concentrated upon the thought and the words that express the thought.

In conclusion two practical suggestions may be made as to this repetition: (1) It has been clearly shown that the best way to memorize a selection is to read and reread it as a whole rather than to break it up into parts and learn each separately.

MEMORY

This law has a limit, of course; but it would apply to any ordinary Bible passage. The old plan of "a verse a day" is both costly and unsatisfactory. It is far better to go over a continuous passage each Sunday for six weeks than to attempt to learn one verse each Sunday. (2) It has been found that it takes fewer repetitions if they are distributed over several days than if they are all concentrated into a single period. The most satisfactory plan is to go over the material several times the first day, a fewer number of times soon afterwards, followed by still briefer periods of study at longer intervals of time. This contributes to permanency of retention at a low cost in time and effort.

These, however, are purely mechanical laws. The most important thing is the understanding. The teacher's task, as far as memory work is concerned, is largely that of helping the pupils to understand and appreciate the material to be memorized.

Questions

1. Point out how memorization of Biblical material helps the individual to better living.

2. What are some of the things that need to be memorized to insure Christian living?

3. What objection have you to asking the pupils to memorize things that have little meaning to them at the time?

4. What are some of the rules to be followed in order to memorize economically?

CHAPTER VIII

MEETING NEW SITUATIONS

Good habits and remembered facts are valuable, but insufficient for living. It has already been suggested that habit has its limitations. Christian living involves the ability to meet new conditions and, confronting these conditions, to do the right thing in the light of definite ideals and guiding principles. As elements in strong Christian character we must recognize adaptability to new situations, the willingness to break away from old habits and old methods when they prove no longer adequate to changed conditions. There is needed too not only the willingness, but the ability. This ability to meet new situations involves two things: (1) The capacity to stop and think, to analyze a situation, to weigh values, and choose wisely. This we have discussed in Chapter V. (2) The possession of definite principles or ideals in the light of which the new situation is estimated and the proper response determined. The Christian life is not a life of habitual performance of routine duties, however worthy. Christianity falls short of adequacy in the institution or the individual if it is unable to apply its principles in new ways to new conditions. The Christian life is a life of consciously guiding principles and ideals. It is only when such principles and ideals become the determining motives in life and work that Christianity is seen at its best. Constant

MEETING NEW SITUATIONS

aspiration and effort to realize and make effective more and more fully these ideals and principles in actual life is an indispensable element in Christian character. The teacher must not neglect the effort to establish in the life definite principles and ideals which may govern when habit fails and falls short of adequacy to new situations.

We may ask now the question, How are such general principles formed and made effective? In trying to answer the question let us examine a particular case.

Generalizing Our Attitudes

A child is confronted with the suffering of another child in the poorer district of his home town. Instinctive sympathy is aroused in him. He is allowed to help by taking needed food and clothing, perhaps by giving something of his own that he values in order to bring happiness to the needy one. Here we have a bond established between the situation, suffering, and the response, helpful actions. Later the child again relieves suffering. The circumstances of the case are altogether different. Here perhaps it may be the needs of children in some foreign land about whom he hears in a story, and he may help in very different ways. But there are common elements in the two cases, suffering and helpfulness. Again and again such instances occur; and, as a result, the response, helpful conduct, comes to be firmly associated, not with any of the accidental circumstances of the particular cases, but with the element common to all, suffering and need. In after life suffering and need, in whatever guise, whatever

71

LEARNING AND TEACHING

the circumstances, will tend to call forth the response of helpfulness. Failure to respond in time would have crushed the sympathetic impulses. Repeated responses have transformed this original prompting into a definite conscious ideal.

Now this illustration indicates to us that the starting point of all our educational endeavor is some instinctive reaction of the learner—in this case sympathy. It is in the child's original nature, as we have already seen, that we have the raw material out of which character must be built. We have no other material with which to work. We note too that what these original impulses lead to depends upon their exercise in appropriate situations and satisfaction resulting from such exercise. Here, then, we have another illustration of the operation of the fundamental laws of learning.

The Law of Analysis

A case of this sort, however, brings out a new feature of the learning process. It shows us how it is possible for right attitudes to be established toward an element that never occurs alone, so that, no matter what the circumstances in which it does occur, it will tend to cause conduct of a definite sort. It is through meeting the element in varying circumstances and responding to it repeatedly that the particular element acquires the power to determine the response made to the total situation, whatever other elements may be in it.

Just here is a point needing special attention. The learner must be conscious of responding to the ele-

72

MEETING NEW SITUATIONS

ment that we are trying to give controlling power. In other words, he must know *why* he is acting as he does, and his reasons must be the right ones. In our illustration the ideal of helpfulness will be formed only when the pupil does acts of kindness in response to his own realization of the suffering and need. If he acts helpfully to please the teacher, or because he enjoys the new sights and experiences of the slum districts, or because his mother tells him to, or because the other pupils do so, it is not the correct association that is being established or the right ideal that is being formed. Unless the pupil has the right motives for his behavior, he may just as likely be developing into a hypocrite who will do his alms before men that he may be seen of them as into a Christian lover of his fellow men.

We have come here upon another of the supplementary principles suggested at the close of Chapter IV. We may, following Thorndike, call this the law of analysis and state it formally as follows: "When any response has been connected with many different situations, alike in the presence of one element and different in other respects, the response is thereby bound to that element; so that when that element appears, even in a very different total situation, it will tend to evoke that response." Understanding the process as it goes on in actual learning is, of course, more important than memorizing an abstract statement of this sort. What we need to see clearly is that it is through the performance of many specific duties that our ideal of duty is formed and that the response to the thought of duty as an element

LEARNING AND TEACHING

in a situation becomes the immediate doing of the duty. The boy who has continually told the truth to parents and to playmates until the ideal of truth telling has become a permanent element in his life will later tell the truth to college professor or employer or business associate. It is through doing many right things, helpful things, unselfish things that considerations of right and helpfulness and unselfishness come to control conduct. It is through doing God's will in this crisis and that, small or great, that God's will comes to have supreme power in the life.

A System of Ideals

The teacher's concern is not, therefore, simply to see that the learner's experience is broadened, his knowledge increased, good conduct secured in certain particular situations, and good habits with reference to these situations firmly established. He must be concerned that in and through all of this there is being built up an organized system of worthy ideals and principles which can govern and control the learner's life whenever crises render specific habits inadequate and conscious control necessary. It is not by the mechanical and artificial securing of correct responses that this is to be accomplished. It is through repeated voluntary choices; it is through constant emphasis upon the importance of stopping to think; it is through repeated experiences in making the right considerations govern; it is through a gradual discovery of relationships between general principles until they finally come to be grouped around one central controlling principle from which

MEETING NEW SITUATIONS

all minor principles derive their value and authority. This is system building, the organization of living.

And it is the work of a lifetime. The process should not be hurried. Our purpose as Sunday-school teachers is to put the Christ life at the center and to make the Christ ideal the controlling ideal. That which should above all else characterize the Christian is the search for God's will for him and the readiness to try to carry out that will in his life. The Christian's crowning ideal is the doing of God's will. Doing right is doing God's will, and every other guiding principle depends upon this one for its value and power. Very early the little child may begin consciously to try to please God and do his will. But the organization of the life around this ideal, the building of character in accord with the pattern given us in the Christ life on earth, is not the work of a day or a year. The well-rounded, thoroughly Christ-imbued character must be builded through a slow process. Each particular decision and choice will contribute toward that end if the pupil himself makes it, of his own free will, in the light of his own constantly enlarging ideal of Jesus and of his own conception of his personal relationship to him as Saviour and Lord.

Questions

1. Mention some cases in which something more than good habits are needed if conduct is to be satisfactory.

2. How do ideals play a part in Christian living?

3. Explain how a person can act in a satisfactory manner in situations which are in many respects quite unlike any that he has met before.

CHAPTER IX

LEARNING FROM OUR ASSOCIATES

OUR study of the process by which we learn has shown us that character is the result of our previous thinking and doing, and that what we think and do is largely the result of our association with other people. We are all born with an interest in human beings and a desire for companionship; but whether we gradually grow more retiring and unwilling to associate with our neighbors or more sociable, finding increasing pleasure in companionship, is largely a matter of training. Some are born with stronger fighting instincts than others, but whether we become lovers of a fight or not depends largely on the kind of people we live with. We are all born with the ability and the tendency to talk, but whether we speak English or French or Chinese depends on the associations of our early childhood.

Particularly clear evidence of the educational effect of the life about us is shown in our tastes for certain foods, a fondness for a special variety of food being peculiar to almost every section of the country. That this liking is not an inborn, unchangeable tendency is shown by the fact that immigrants soon develop a taste for the characteristic foods of the land of their adoption. Similar evidence is found in our habits of dress.

We have evidence also of the effect of education in the moral aspects of life. One part of the world

LEARNING FROM OUR ASSOCIATES

lines up for the defense of autocracy, while most of the other nations engage in a determined fight to make democracy the law of the world. It is clear that the spirit of autocracy is not something that is born in every individual of the autocratic nations. In fact, we see quite clearly that the German spirit of unquestioned obedience to the State is the product of the social life and particularly of the educational system of the nation.

Heredity and Environment

We often hear debates on the relative importance of heredity and environment. It is not necessary here to come to a decision as to which plays a larger part in the making of life. The point to be emphasized is that each is very important and that the two work together to fashion character. The individual is born with an equipment of instinctive tendencies that form the foundation for his whole life, but the direction and development of these tendencies depends upon his contact with the life about him.

Imitation

We sometimes say that the influence of each individual over his fellows is due to the universal human tendency to imitate. This is not quite correct, for we have no such universal tendency. If our neighbor plants a particular kind of seed and his crop turns out to be a failure, we do not rush to imitate him. If he drinks from a certain well and soon after contracts typhoid fever, we do not hasten to follow his example. Instead, then, of saying that we

LEARNING AND TEACHING

imitate every one about us, it would be more correct to say that we learn from all of our acquaintances. We watch their ways of doing things; and if we think that we can get the things we want in the way that they get the things they want, we follow their way of acting. We do the things they do if their experience seems to indicate to us that following their example would be to our profit. We take their advice when we believe that the method they urge is the worth-while method.

Social Approval

Not only are we guided by the experience of others; we are influenced by their attitude. Social approval and disapproval are probably the strongest forces in the control of our lives. They even outweigh man's desire to preserve his life, for men will often gladly die rather than act in a way that society does not approve. We have all known children who tearfully protested against having to wear a certain kind of clothing that was an occasion for fun-making on the part of their playmates. The mental suffering of a child under such circumstances is certainly not less than that of a man who might find himself under the necessity of wearing a straw hat in winter or a red tie to a funeral, or of the woman whose only coat is several seasons out of style. Undoubtedly both society and the individuals of whom it is composed are often wrong in their judgment and sacrifice the greater to the lesser good, but the fact remains that to violate social custom takes more courage than most people possess.

LEARNING FROM OUR ASSOCIATES

Influence of Special Groups

While we learn from all our acquaintances and can truly say, "I am a part of all that I have met," we receive the largest influences from certain special groups. We may lay down the principle that intimacy or acquaintanceship is a determining factor in social education. For this reason the family has an important influence in the shaping of the lives of its members. The particular bent of character of an individual depends to a large extent on the kind of home in which he has grown up. From the earliest days the child learns from his parents and the other members of the household. We often say that a child is born with a certain disposition because we find the same characteristic in his father or his mother. It would probably more often be correct to say that the child learned this habit of life in his early years in the home. Many of the things that are passed on from parent to child come not by what we usually call heredity, but by what we might better call education.

In boy life especially the voluntary group, or "gang," is another well-known agency in the fashioning of character either for good or for ill. To a certain extent it deliberately undertakes to school the new member into its ways, but for the most part its educational work is informal and incidental. The boy "picks up" the ways of his companions.

Prison life has long been acknowledged to have a powerful influence over the lives of prisoners. It is commonly agreed that to place youthful offenders in the companionship of hardened criminals is almost

LEARNING AND TEACHING

certain to hinder rather than help the reformation of character of the younger people.

The number of groups that participate in the molding of the character of one individual is often large. The saloon and its associations, the baseball team, the political party, the group of fellow workers in shop—all of the associations of everyday life contribute to make the individual something other than he was without them.

Possibly some may say that a large proportion of our learning comes from books and that this educational means is primarily individualistic and not social. A little thought, however, will reveal the fact that the influence is really social, for books are merely avenues by which there come to us the experiences and thoughts of their writers.

The School and Its Purpose

It is because of this possibility of learning from others that we have what we call educational institutions. We see that as children come into relationship with others their lives are changed, and we determine that their teachers shall be chosen not merely at random, but shall be those who will help to produce *desirable* changes in the young lives. We select from our number certain individuals with large experience and say to them: "Go, live with the children and be their teachers."

But we must remember that the children learn not only from the teachers, but from their classmates. Possibly what they learn on the school playground affects the fundamental things of character as much

LEARNING FROM OUR ASSOCIATES

as what they learn in the classroom. University graduates, in recounting the benefits of university life, often speak of their association with their fellow students as of as much importance as their academic work.

The Value of the Class

Therefore, when we form a class of pupils in day school or in Sunday school, we are not simply bringing together a group of people that the time of the teacher may be economized, so that he can with one repetition bring to the attention of a large group as much material as he could bring in the same time to a single individual. The class itself is an educational agency, and the members of it learn from one another as well as from the teacher. We sometimes hear it said that the ideal class would consist of one teacher and one pupil. Certainly there are advantages in individual instruction, but the one-pupil class is not by any means ideal. Individual instruction has very serious limitations.

During recent years much emphasis has been placed on the importance of having organized classes, especially in the young people's and adult sections of the school. Some have thought that the chief advantage of the organized class lies in the larger interest awakened. This is far from correct. The chief advantage to be derived from class organization lies in the educational possibilities of the social group. The class whose organization exists not merely on paper, but whose members form a real co-operative group, is able to undertake tasks that are beyond the range of the class that is a mere collec-

LEARNING AND TEACHING

tion of individuals. This practical experience in co-operative effort for common purposes is of the utmost educational importance.

We often forget that we cannot be Christian alone, that Christian living involves living together. The Great Commandment requires not only love of God, but love of our fellow man. The class group permits that intimacy of association and effort that makes possible practice in real Christian living. The educational value of the social group is high, and careful efforts should be made to develop such a spirit of real social living that the maximum results in this direction may be obtained.

Questions

1. Mention at least six things that you have learned from other people.

2. Can you think of any knowledge or ability that you possess in the attainment of which other people had no share?

3. Mention some cases that have come to your notice where persons have "imitated" their associates. Point out in each case what seemed to be the reason for the "imitation."

4. What evidence can you produce to show the educational importance of the voluntary group or "gang"?

5. Suggest some ways in which the "gang" may be used to secure educationally valuable results.

6. From what you have learned of the influence of the social group in the building of character, how large an educational factor would you consider "school spirit" to be?

CHAPTER X

THE TEACHER'S TASK AND RESOURCES

THE earlier chapters of this book have been devoted almost entirely to a discussion of the pupil and the learning process. Little has been said regarding the teacher and his work. This emphasis was deliberate and, we think, justifiable. The only final and satisfactory test of the success of the work of the school is the progress made by the pupil. Our interest is not so much in how the teacher is to teach as in how the pupil is to develop. If the young people in our care are becoming more truly Christian in their whole living, we are justified in feeling that their education is proceeding in the right direction. If our teaching is contributing to that progress, then we may conclude that our methods are good. When we turn our attention to the teaching process, we should remember, therefore, that it must never be thought of as apart from the learning process, but as simply another aspect of the matter that we have already discussed.

The Teacher's Part

The work of the teacher is needed for two reasons. One is that the teacher can hasten the learning process and so economize the pupil's time. Every child is born into the world with certain abilities and tendencies; but if he were thrown entirely on his own resources, he would grow up, if he did not per-

LEARNING AND TEACHING

ish in the process, more ignorant and helpless than most of the animals. By the method of trial and error he would accumulate some knowledge as to the best ways to do certain things, but his learning would be slow and expensive. We teach our children in order that they may be saved from as much as possible of this toilsome process. We place at their disposal our accumulated experience and the experience of other people. As an example of the results of this method, we have the fact that by careful teaching we are able to introduce boys and girls still in their teens to higher mathematics. Under such guidance young men become skilled mechanics. With the help of an instructor, the college student in a few weeks or days works through a philosophic system that represents the life work of one of the world's intellectual giants.

Education is sometimes defined as the effort of one generation to pass on its inheritance to the next generation. Something is lost, of course, in the process of transmission, but nevertheless much is saved, and so progress is possible.

The Control of Learning

The other reason for the teacher's work is that guidance is needed if development is to take place in the right direction. We are not judged by the amount of knowledge and ability in our possession, but by the *kind* of knowledge and ability that is ours. It has sometimes been said that the aim of education is "the harmonious development of all one's abilities." We find, however, that our pupils

THE TEACHER'S TASK AND RESOURCES

have abilities to cheat, to lie, to quarrel; and our task as educators is not to help these powers to develop, but to check them or to turn the energy back of them into other activities. The good teacher, therefore, not only helps his pupils to rapid thinking, but teaches them an appreciation of the most worth-while things.

The Pupils

For the accomplishment of this important task there are at the disposal of the teacher several valuable resources. *There is the pupil himself.* The teacher is sometimes tempted to wish that John or Jim or perhaps May or Elsie would stay at home for this and several future Sundays; but, after all, these very individuals have in them the making of fully developed Christians. The restlessness which sometimes threatens the orderliness of the class is an evidence of the pent-up motive power that may be used to do great things. It may easily be a nuisance, and it will surely be dangerous if it does not find outlet in useful activities; but without it there would be only stagnation and decay. Of all the precious elements of which the teacher may make use, the pupil's activity stands first in importance.

Then *there is the possibility of change in the pupils.* They are what they are because of many things —because of their inheritance from their parents and from their more remote ancestors, and because of the homes and communities in which they have lived. Heredity is indeed important, and we may be glad that our pupils have inherited so many fine qualities; but we must not despair because they

LEARNING AND TEACHING

have inherited also some undesirable traits. There is always the possibility of change. Our pupils, whether children or adults, are not what they were nor what they will be. Both children and adults are plastic. They may become better, or they may become worse; but, at any rate, they will change. Heredity has been to many a needlessly great and terrible bugbear.

How Changes Occur

Furthermore, we have seen that the *changes do not occur in a haphazard fashion, but are according to laws.* These laws are sometimes quite complex and often hard to understand, but they are definite. We have seen that there are certain ways in which we get new ideas and in which the new and old are associated. We have also seen that there are certain rules for the formation of habits and that only by using these rules can we build up the habits we wish to have. *It is by using and not by fighting the laws of living that we can control life.* It thus appears that the fact that growth is according to law is not an obstacle, but is a real advantage to the teacher.

A further resource at the disposal of the teacher is the fact that somehow *human nature responds to the good.* Other things being equal, we choose the better, not the worse. It is when life is distorted and spoiled or when we do not stop to think that we take the worse thing and neglect the better. The teaching of Jesus shows this very clearly. He saw divine possibilities in man. He was confident that where lives were not deliberately hardened and made

THE TEACHER'S TASK AND RESOURCES

unreceptive the truth would find entrance and men would choose the right. Because of this confidence he taught and preached, he counseled and reproved, all that his hearers might have a chance.

Agencies of Religious Education

Another resource of great value is *the environment in which our pupils live.* Many of them come from Christian homes. All have lived in communities where at least some of the people have been worthy followers of the Master. In our last chapter we discussed the value of the social group and saw that the home, the school, the playground, and the shop all contribute to the education of the individual.

Still another resource of the teacher is his *message.* Perhaps this has been better recognized than some other things, but we must watch carefully lest we give it anything less than its full place. We have always made the Bible, and especially the life of Jesus, central in our work, and rightly so. We must continue so to do, for it is a message of life in its fullness and permanency. And while we think of our message, we must not fail to think of the whole of it. The whole spiritual inheritance of the race is at the disposal of teacher and pupil. The long, long story of how successive generations of men and women and boys and girls have struggled with difficulties and doubts and temptations, have gathered strength and won victories, is available for our guidance and inspiration. The fact that we find Christianity in the lives of men and in the books they have written

87

LEARNING AND TEACHING

makes us love the Bible and its message not less, but more. It is a living witness to the fact that the teaching of the Bible is able to transform life and make it beautiful and good.

The Influence of Personality

Finally, the teacher has the advantage that the great source of growth is *the touch of life on life*. From childhood we have heard of the "tremendous influence of personality." We have been advised to "shun evil companions" and to seek the company of the good. We have been assured, and we have assured others, that we cannot mingle with our fellows without being influenced by their lives and in turn having an influence over them.

Two points need to be emphasized in our thought of the influence of personality. One is that personality can be improved. The teacher who comes to his work weary and worn by the toil or even the merrymaking of the day before cannot possibly do his best work. The teacher owes it, as a duty to the pupils and to the school, to come to his work not tired and nervous, but rested and in the best possible physical health. Our work would probably be more efficient if we required all of our teachers regularly to pass a physical examination by a competent medical examiner.

The matter of personal appearance should not be forgotten. The teacher should be a practical demonstration of the fact that there are things worth more than extravagance in clothing, but neatness is needed if the teacher is to command that respect of the pupils essential to successful teaching.

THE TEACHER'S TASK AND RESOURCES

So much emphasis has been placed on a high type of character on the part of the teacher that only the great importance of the point justifies a further reference to it. If the teacher states in the class session that tobacco has the effect of reducing physical efficiency and then indulges in smoking, the pupils will very naturally discount what he has said. We well know that what a person does is a better index to his beliefs than what he says, and even young children are not ignorant of this fact. The teacher's practice must harmonize with his precepts, or his words are of little value. The teacher whose daily life is regulated by the rule of Christ, whose words and deeds are marked by a truly religious spirit, will be a constant source of inspiration and guidance to his pupils.

In the knowledge that personality can be improved there is a challenge to every prospective teacher. Some shrink from teaching because, as they say, they lack the right personality. This is not an adequate exemption plea. While some by nature or by previous training possess special qualifications for teaching, there are few who cannot by careful thought and effort develop the ability to do useful work.

This thought leads to the other word of caution that must be spoken in a consideration of the topic of personality. This is that neither inherited nor acquired personal characteristics can take the place of hard and continuous work. For the work of teaching there should be thorough general preparation in advance, and there should be intensive study

89

LEARNING AND TEACHING

for each week's work. Neither ability, popularity, nor previous success can guarantee good work. Special preparation is essential.

Questions

1. Why is the work of the teacher important? Make a list of the chief reasons.

2. What use can the teacher make of the pupil's desire for activity?

3. In what ways does the community in which you live contribute to the moral uplift of its young people?

4. Mention some of the essential qualifications of a successful Sunday-school teacher.

CHAPTER XI

UNDERSTANDING THE PUPIL A FIRST ESSENTIAL

A TEACHER takes charge of a new class. One of his pupils is Edward Smith. Edward Smith is red-headed, freckle-faced, and barefooted. His eyes dance with mischief, and he can't keep still two minutes at a time to save his life. He is a very live, active, mischievous, lovable youngster. What will the teacher do for him? What will all that vitality and activity, that mischief and that loveliness lead to in the boy's life and character during the years ahead? This is a very real problem to his teacher. The big question is, "What can I do for Edward Smith?" But before he can answer this question he must first ask, "What does Edward Smith need?" And this leads to asking first of all, "What kind of a boy is Edward Smith?"

Knowing the Pupils

Answering this question about his pupil means not only knowing certain things about Edward Smith, but understanding those things and so understanding the boy himself. The teacher will realize that he can get much help in understanding Edward Smith if he learns something about boys in general and boys of the age of Edward Smith in particular. So, while he keeps as close to Edward Smith as he can and finds out as much about him as possible, he also reviews what he has learned about the characteristics

LEARNING AND TEACHING

of ten-year-old boys; or he turns to some one who has studied ten-year-old boys and can tell him what they are usually like. He learns that in ten-year-old boys the "acquisitive feeling" is strong; that rivalry and emulation are effective motives; that there is a keen sense of justice, at least as it relates to themselves; that the sense of reality and certainty is developing; that boys of this age are interested in the "use" of things; they love puzzles; they are interested in the doings and sayings of grown people; "chumming" is a strong tendency, and the influence of companions is dominant, and so on. Then what?

The teacher's next question will be, Is Edward Smith like this? In some ways Edward Smith may seem very different from this typical ten-year-old boy. But doubtless he will exhibit most of the general traits that are characteristic of that particular stage of development. The teacher's next question is, then, How shall I use these tendencies, these activities, these interests in helping Edward Smith? Can I make use of his acquisitive tendency so that it will lead to the collection of useful things and develop into a just sense of property instead of becoming selfish and miserly? Rivalry and emulation are strong motives. Can I get him to try to surpass his own record, to rival his own past self rather than selfishly to endeavor to beat others? I must be careful to be just and to make him see that I am just. Can I develop in him the desire for justice for others as well as for himself? His sense of reality is developing. I must, therefore, discard imaginative illustrations and use illustrations from

UNDERSTANDING THE PUPIL

nature, from personal experience from the lives of men who command his respect. This boy of ten asks, "What is a thing good for? What is the use?" I must make him see that it pays to do right. He loves puzzles. Instead of giving him information I will make him hunt for the answers to questions and the solutions of problems. Since he is interested in grown people, I must use illustrations and stories about grown people and must try to show him how his conduct will affect his life as a grown man.

But Edward Smith seems in many ways a law unto himself. No such generalizations as the teacher finds in a book seem exactly to describe him or to fit his case. Many helpful suggestions as to traits to look for and ways of dealing with them may be obtained from books, but study of books about boys will never be of itself sufficient. The teacher must study Edward Smith himself; and not only Edward, but Edward's father and mother and Edward's home, his chores and his games, his school and his playground, the streets he walks through and the boys and girls he plays with. Only thus can the teacher really understand Edward and so answer the questions "What does Edward need?" and "How can I help him?" For it is only through understanding Edward that his needs can be known; and, further, as we shall see, it is only through understanding Edward that one can know how to go about helping him.

Individual Differences

And the teacher has not only Edward to help. Here are John and James and Albert and George

LEARNING AND TEACHING

and the others. They are all alike in many ways, and yet how different in so many other ways! They were different to start with; and different homes, different training, different schools, different companions, different work, and different play have confirmed and increased the differences in personality and character. The teacher will need to know each one as a person, as an individual. And while this teacher of boys is wrestling with his problems, over here is a teacher of girls of the same age, perhaps, but presenting different problems because they are girls. The first task of each of these teachers and of all teachers is to know and understand the pupils intrusted to him. These pupils are active, interested, growing, and have hungry bodies and minds. Their needs must be met, their activities directed, their lives controlled, organized, guided. Some of their activities must be encouraged. Some of their interests must be cultivated; some must be guided along new lines; some must be discouraged or suppressed. The teacher wishes to help. Understanding the pupils is the first step in finding out how to help them.

Scientific Child Study

We may say, then, speaking in general terms, that it is important, first, for the teacher to be thoroughly familiar with the general characteristics to be expected at the stage of development in which he finds his pupils. Careful, patient observers of child life have been able to describe many of the general characteristics of each of the various periods of development, and few things can profit the teacher more

94

UNDERSTANDING THE PUPIL

than the study of some of the excellent summaries of the results of scientific child study. We may here simply urge the primary importance of the teacher's knowing the pupils. What we shall teach and how we shall teach are dependent at every step upon the pupil's interests and spontaneous activities as these reveal his needs and capacities. It should be evident that no teacher can teach without knowing his pupils—what they are interested in and what they do, their likes and dislikes, their peculiar capacities and needs and dangers. But this knowledge, it hardly need be said, cannot be had solely from books, however reliable. In the second place, then, the teacher must be himself a first-hand student of child life. Especially must he study the lives of the particular children intrusted to his care. No two pupils are alike. No generalization can be trusted implicitly in its application to the individual. Generalizations can serve only as guides in the study of individuals, as standards by which individual variations are to be estimated. The teacher must not be content simply with knowing something of the general facts about the stage of life in which his pupils are. He must know his pupils as individuals, as personalities, with all the queer twists and quirks and divergences from the normal that each personality may present. He should neglect no opportunity to learn all he can of the home life, the previous training, the day school, and the out-of-school activities and experiences of the pupils. Every bit of such knowledge is worth storing up. At any minute it may shed its revealing light upon some

LEARNING AND TEACHING

otherwise mysterious perversity or stupidity and point the way out of the difficulties presented. Books about children, the conclusions and summaries of trained and expert observers, are not to be scoffed at. They are a necessity. They will prove a boon and a blessing to any teacher who will use them. But they are meant to help only. They are not and never will be all-sufficient. They can help to an understanding of one's own pupils; they can never take the place of such understanding.

All this is not demanding too much of the teacher. It is setting the ideal high. But this is well. No teacher with sincere purpose and readiness to serve should allow lack of technical knowledge and training to stand in the way or serve as an excuse for shirking duty. But, taking up the work in the spirit of genuine service, certainly he should use every means that time and energy permit to improve his teaching by increasing his knowledge of child nature in general and of his pupils in particular, so that with knowledge of subject matter may go knowledge of the ways in which that subject matter may find lodgment in the minds of his pupils and influence their lives and mold their characters in conformity to the great pattern and ideal of all Christian living—the life of the Master himself.

Questions

1. Consider the boy or girl that you know best and write down a list of the things he or she is most interested in. Make a list also of the most conspicuous traits of this child. Now turn to "Life in the Making" or some other book about child nature and compare your lists with the

UNDERSTANDING THE PUPIL

accounts you find there. How do they agree? In what respects do they differ?

2. Compare this boy or girl with other boys and girls of the same age that you know. What traits and interests do you discover to be common to all of the group? In what ways does this particular boy or girl you are studying seem exceptional?

3. Which of the peculiar traits of the child can you explain as due to definite features of his home environment or early training? Can you explain some of the ground of heredity? Can you find other explanations for still other traits?

4. What are suggested to you as the special needs of the boy or girl you are studying?

5. Can you think of ways to use the special interests of this boy or girl in meeting his needs and so helping him to learn in the true sense?

CHAPTER XII

THE TEST OF TEACHING MATERIAL

The test of teaching is the change it produces in the lives of learners. Better living, straighter thinking, nobler feeling, more worthy conduct—these we have a right to expect as results of good teaching. But sometimes teaching fails to produce the results hoped for. Why?

The Use of Language

Perhaps you have at some time listened to a lecturer who was speaking a foreign language. You were giving close attention. And the lecturer was talking sense. Yet you got absolutely nothing from what he said; his words could not possibly influence your life. You did not know the language. In other words, you lacked the knowledge or experience that would enable you to understand and apply what was being said.

Perhaps, again, you have been in a classroom where the pupils were quiet and attentive and the teacher was speaking sensibly and well. But you felt sure the pupils were not understanding what the teacher was saying and that in consequence their lives were not being influenced by his words. He was talking over their heads. They were getting his meaning very little better than if he had been using a foreign language. Why? Because they lacked the experience, the knowledge necessary for

98

THE TEST OF TEACHING MATERIAL

the understanding of the words he was using. Their lives were not influenced, because what was said did not come close enough to them for them to understand it and act upon it.

These examples bring out clearly for us one reason why some of our teaching fails to produce results. What one does not understand can have no influence upon him. Moreover, it is equally true that what one understands wrongly will influence him wrongly. If we mean one thing by our words and our pupils think that we mean something quite different, we may influence their lives; but it will not be in the way that we intended. It is not what the teacher says, but what the pupils get out of what he says, that counts. It is not what the teacher means, but what the pupils think he means that is important. It is not what the *teacher* thinks or feels or does, but what the *pupil* thinks or feels or does, that determines results in teaching.

We may say, then, that the pupil's ability rightly to understand the new experience we try to give him through our words or in other ways is necessary if our teaching is really to influence his life. The man who knows nothing of French gets no help from a lecture in that language. Neither does the boy get help from us when we use big words and deal in ideas that lie entirely outside the range of his experience. We are wasting words to urge a boy to "act in the complex relationships with his fellows as considerations of humanity, self-abnegation, and altruism require." But this same boy would understand

99

LEARNING AND TEACHING

and respond to the idea of fair play or of "giving the other fellow a square deal."

The Value of Experience

We must talk in terms that our pupils can understand if we expect our teaching to influence their lives. And the ability of our pupils to understand and respond properly to the new experience we try to give them depends upon their past experience. It is the knowledge acquired through past experience that determines what new experiences shall mean. A little child, seeing a picture of a rat for the first time, calls it a "bunny." It looks like a "bunny." She knows that name. But she has had no experience with rats. She interprets this new experience in terms of her past experience—by means of what she already knows. It would be possible to find many amusing examples of the fact that words and things very often mean to a little child something quite different from what they mean for us. A little child quoted one of the Beatitudes: "Blessed are the shoemakers." He heard the word "peacemakers"; but his knowledge was insufficient to give him any correct idea, and so the idea established in his mind was one closely related to something that he did know. Bolton gives us the illustration of the child who heard the verse, "A double-minded man is unstable in all his ways," and rendered it thus: "A double-minded man is in the stable all the time." Again, the child who heard the statement that a hen lays on an average three eggs a week later defined "average" as "what a hen lays on." James tells us

THE TEST OF TEACHING MATERIAL

that the sail of a boat is called a curtain by the child. His "child of two played for a week with the first orange that was given him, calling it a 'ball.' He called the first whole eggs he saw 'potatoes,' having been accustomed to see his 'eggs' broken in a glass and his potatoes without the skin. A folding pocket corkscrew he unhesitatingly called 'bad scissors.'"

And it is not only in experiences with children that we find illustrations of the fact that what words or things mean to us depends upon our past experience, for this is a general law of the mental life. What the word "river" means for you depends upon your past experience with rivers. "Watts" and "ohms" and "volts" and "amperes" are words that have definite meaning for the electrical engineer; for the ordinary man they are meaningless, or the meaning that they have is very vague. The twenty-third Psalm means very much more to the man who understands the relationship between the shepherd and his sheep in ancient Palestine than it does to the man who knows only of sheep-herding on a Western ranch. To the man who never saw or heard of a sheep the Psalm would mean little. How much more would the phrase "the shadow of a rock in a weary land" mean to the man familiar with desert stretches than to the dweller in a land of hills and valleys and trees and grass and flowing streams! A savage in Africa would probably prefer a gaudy bit of painted glass to a twenty-dollar gold piece. He has no experience to indicate to him the meaning or the value of the coin.

LEARNING AND TEACHING

The "Set" of the Mind

What things mean to us is, then, determined by our past experience. But there is another factor that helps to determine what an experience means and how it influences action. A teacher writes on the board $\frac{4}{2}$ and asks for the result. The pupil's reply will depend, of course, upon what he has learned of arithmetic. But it will depend also upon whether he looks upon the example as an example in addition or subtraction or multiplication. The purpose, the attitude, the mental "set" at the time helps to determine the meaning of the figures and the response given to the question. Consider how differently one regards a flower when strolling aimlessly and when on a botanizing expedition. The difference is not in the flower nor in the person's past experience. It lies wholly in his "set," his attitude, his purpose at the time. The word "cross" means very different things in the following sentences: "The consecrated cross I'll bear;" "In the cross of Christ I glory;" "Let us cross over the river and rest under the shade of the trees;" "He is a dangerous person to cross;" "The child is cross." The variations in the meaning of the word depend not on one's past experience, not on any change in the word itself, but upon a different mental attitude determined by the different contexts in which the word occurs. Suppose the proof sheets of a book come back to the author in bad condition. The sheets are a mass of misspelling and misplaced punctuation marks and badly spaced lines and words; it is these things that he sees as he reads proof. But he may

THE TEST OF TEACHING MATERIAL

read over the same material to discover how well he has expressed the thought he wished to convey. The pages then become a very different thing: his attention is now centered on the thought. What the lines of print mean to him depends in large measure upon the purpose with which he reads them.

If the teacher tells the story of David and Goliath to a boy who is thinking of a new sling he made yesterday, the boy is apt to seize upon David's skill as a wielder of the sling rather than his courageous manliness. And his response will probably be a question about how David made his sling or how big were the rocks he threw or how long he had to practice before he could throw so well. He may, even, after Sunday school try to emulate David's prowess as a marksman. There is nothing wrong with the boy's interest in these things. But the teacher is not accomplishing what he wishes. And it is not because the boy is unable to understand and admire courage. It is because his frame of mind, when he hears the story, causes him to respond to a different part of it than was intended by the teacher. The pupil who was asked, "Where was St. Paul converted?" gave a perfectly correct answer when he said: "In the ninth chapter of Acts." The trouble was simply that he answered from a "background of textual reference," as the author who gives the illustration puts it, while the teacher asked the question from a "geographical background," expecting the answer "On the road to Damascus." The mental attitude of the pupil was different from that of the teacher, and so the question meant something different for him.

103

LEARNING AND TEACHING

This principle of the influence of past experience and of present mental attitude in determining the meaning of a new experience, and hence the nature of response to it, is familiar to many teachers as the principle of apperception. Thorndike has said: "Nine-tenths of teaching illustrates the use or abuse of the law of apperception."

Some Rules for Teachers

The practical suggestions that follow for the teacher from this fundamental law of learning are evident. For our teaching to be effective our pupils must be able to understand and respond properly to the new experience we bring to them. How they will understand and respond depends upon their past experience and upon their present frame of mind. How, then, can the teacher be sure that his teaching will be effective? By making sure that his pupils have the experience that will enable them to understand and respond as he wishes and by getting them in the frame of mind that will insure understanding and response.

First of all, then, the teacher must know his pupils: what they already know and what they can do; their daily lives at home and in school and on the streets; their studies, the movie shows they see, the games they play, the chores they do. Only with such knowledge can the teacher know what his pupils are able to understand.

Then, knowing these things about his pupils, the teacher must ask about everything he plans to say and do: "From what I know of my pupils, what will

THE TEST OF TEACHING MATERIAL

this mean to them? How will it affect them?" Here is a noble thought, a beautiful story, an impressive illustration; but will its nobility be felt by Edward Smith? Will he be able to understand it, to catch its true significance? Will the hero of the story seem a "sissy" to him? Or will the situation in which the hero finds himself be so utterly unlike anything Edward Smith knows about that he will miss the lesson entirely? Will this exquisite poetry carry its message to the twelve-year-old girl in my class? Or will it fail because she "don't like poetry, anyhow"?

A point that the Sunday-school teacher needs especially to guard is the use of symbolism that the grown person can understand, but that the little child takes quite literally. One little boy, Kirkpatrick tells us, declared that he didn't want to be Jesus's little lamb because then he would "have to eat grass." A little girl was sorely troubled over the "river of life" in the New Jerusalem of St. John's vision because she knew of no body of water into which it could flow. But then she heard of the "great gulf" fixed between Dives and Lazarus in Abraham's bosom. Of course the river flowed into the gulf, and she was satisfied.

Again, in our use of objects as illustrations there is great danger of our expecting too much of children in the way of making comparisons and spiritual applications. The evangelist who, in preaching to children, displays a big rat trap and compares the way in which it lures and catches rats with the way in which sin lures and catches children doubt-

LEARNING AND TEACHING

less gets his hearers interested. But the chances are that they are interested in the trap and the rats and the dramatic story he tells and not in the moral and spiritual application he wishes to make.

Every bit of our teaching material must, then, be viewed from the standpoint of the pupils and in relation to their limited experience. Until we have at least tried to bring it to this test, we are not justified in attempting to use it. And, let it be emphasized, we cannot even make the attempt unless we know our pupils.

Finally, the teacher cannot be content with simply knowing what his pupils can understand. He must take steps to insure the proper frame of mind for the reception of the new experience. He must call into mind those things in the pupil's past experience that are most closely related to this new experience. He must "get the point of contact"; he must "proceed from the known to the related unknown"; and the "unknown" new experience must not be presented until the proper "old" is present in mind to take hold of the new and lend it meaning and value.

Questions

1. "To ask teachers in the Primary and Beginners' Departments to teach a consecutive series of lessons from the Gospel of John, or from the Acts and the Epistles, is pedagogically absurd." (Meyer.) Why?

2. On the basis of the principles suggested in this chapter, criticize the plan of using the same lesson material for all members of the Sunday school, regardless of age or previous instruction.

3. Consider the suitability of these lessons for a class of boys ten or twelve years old: "The Word Made Flesh"

106

THE TEST OF TEACHING MATERIAL

(John i. 1-18); "Jesus and the Woman of Samaria" (John iv. 1-42); "Jesus the Bread of Life" (John vi. 22-51); "Jesus Anointed at Bethany" (John xii. 1-11).

4. Recall some lessons that you have taught or have heard taught and think over such questions as these about them: (1) Were the words used and the ideas presented such that the pupils could understand them? (2) Were the pupils in a proper frame of mind to understand them? (3) Was definite effort made to relate them to the actual experiences of the pupils' lives? To get the pupils into the proper frame of mind?

CHAPTER XIII

GETTING AND HOLDING THE PUPIL'S ATTENTION

THE teacher must have the attention of his pupils if he is to teach at all. He must have the undivided attention of his class if he is to teach well. If the pupil's attention is somewhere else, the pupil himself might just as well be somewhere else. The teacher's time and energy are wasted or worse, for either the pupil is getting nothing at all or he is getting wrong impressions and distorted notions and is being established in the habit of inattention. This habit confirmed in the pupils will, says Dr. Fitch, "prevent them from ever becoming thoughtful readers, diligent observers, and earnest listeners as long as they live."

This brings us to the question, "How can we get and hold the attention of our pupils?" Or, better, "How *should* we get and hold the attention of our pupils?" For there may be more than one way in which we *can* do it. We want to find the *best* way— that is, the way that is most valuable educationally.

Attention and Interest

The best way—in fact, the only way—to get attention to arouse interest. The child attends to that in which he is interested. Spontaneous attention corresponds to immediate interest; voluntary attention, to remote interest—that is, interest

GETTING AND HOLDING ATTENTION

in some future achievement to which the present activity contributes. For younger pupils we are forced to depend upon the first; with older pupils we can expect the latter. Voluntary attention is almost an impossibility for the little tots; for older pupils it should be expected only as a result of interest in some ultimate purpose to which the lesson contributes. Attention and interest are two sides of the same process. Interest is the motive; attention is the resultant state of mind. If we can get our pupils genuinely interested, we may be sure that the attentive attitude, whole-souled effort and activity, mental and physical, genuine absorption in what is being said or done will be the result. And such absorption, such undivided attention and effort alone can insure efficient learning and permanent influence on life and character.

The answer to the question, "How may the teacher get and hold the attention of his pupil?" is, then, the discussion of interest and motive. The question boils down to one of choice between different motives, between different interests that may be appealed to.

Eliminating Distractions

It is well for the teacher, first, to bear in mind that what we call inattention usually means attention to something else. The pupil is practically always attending to something. The teacher's task, then, is to get the attention directed to the right thing. "The teacher's task is to outbid some rival. Attention is not a quantity to be created, but a force to be directed."

LEARNING AND TEACHING

Care should be taken, then, in so far as possible, to remove all distractions. Everything that has a chance to draw the pupil's attention away, to get him thinking about something else, adds to the difficulty of the teacher's task. As many such things as possible should be guarded against in advance. For this reason it is best to have a separate room for each class. The furnishings and pictures of the classroom should relate to the work to be done. The room should be cut off from outside noises; away from the street, if possible. Attention should be given to the lighting, the heating, and the ventilation of the room. Genuine physical discomfort is bound to interfere with attention. After the lesson is begun nothing should be allowed to interrupt it. Preparing the records, taking the collection, distributing the literature, etc., should all be attended to before or after the study of the lesson, better at the beginning. At any rate, a definite time should be set aside, and these things should not be allowed to distract attention from the lesson. Interferences from outside should not be permitted. There should be a definite understanding that the teacher is not to be interrupted in the midst of a lesson. The time is all too short at best: every moment must be made to count. On this point Weigle aptly says: "A superintendent may mean well, yet strut about importantly and confer with this person or that in more or less audible tones till he creates more disorder and inattention than he can ever correct with the bell that he uses for that purpose."

GETTING AND HOLDING ATTENTION

Good Teaching

With distraction guarded against, the question of getting and holding the attention is chiefly a question of good teaching. Good teaching means, among other things: A lesson adapted to the capacities, interests, and needs of the pupils; careful preparation to the point of mastery; careful planning, in the light of what the teacher knows of his individual pupils, toward a definite end to be accomplished by the lesson; genuine interest and earnestness on the part of the teacher; alertness and ability to use unexpected opportunities that may arise in the course of the discussion of the lesson; enlisting the activity of the pupils and stimulating them to thought and expression; variety; the use of those special methods that are best adapted to pupils of different ages. These special methods are discussed in other chapters. In studying these later chapters it is well to bear in mind that acquiring the ability to use these methods effectively is a long step in the direction of solving the teacher's problem of holding the attention of his pupils. Demanding attention is a poor way of securing it. Attention so given will soon wander elsewhere, and before long the demand itself will go unheeded. The ideal is to teach in such a way that the interest of the pupil is aroused, and thus his attention is gripped and held.

Interest in the Lesson

If the lesson is interesting, we may be sure that the pupils will attend to it. But a caution is needed here. "It is not enough to simply have attention,"

111

LEARNING AND TEACHING

says Thorndike; "it must be attention to the right thing." Perhaps the principle that the lesson must be "interesting" to the pupil has in the past met with more general recognition in the Sunday school than elsewhere. It has been largely under the necessity of holding its pupils in the school through keeping them interested. As a result the risk that the Sunday-school teacher runs, the error into which many have fallen, is that of making the interest to which he appeals external and superficial rather than intrinsic and vital, reliance upon artificial devices and excitement rather than upon sound method and the engaging of the pupil's real and deeper self. There is danger in the practice of *making* a lesson interesting and exciting "interest" through the use of all sorts of devices that attract attention. If the interest of the pupil is not interest in the lesson itself, it is valueless. We must, first of all, have a lesson that can interest the pupil, and then all that is necessary is that it be given a chance to make its own appeal. "I know," Dewey writes, "of no more demoralizing doctrine, when taken literally, than the assertion . . . that *after* subject matter has been selected *then* the teacher should make it interesting." And again: "When things have to be *made* interesting, it is because interest itself is wanting. Moreover, the phrase itself is a misnomer. The thing, the object is no more interesting than it was before. The appeal is simply made to the child's love of pleasure. He is excited in a given direction with the hope that somehow or other during this excitation he will assimilate something otherwise repulsive."

112

GETTING AND HOLDING ATTENTION

When we rely upon artificial devices—objects and "chalk" stories, catchy tricks, funny stories, mimicry, fascinating pictures, anything that appeals to a child's love of sensation and excitement in order to "get his attention"—there is danger of centering his attention upon these devices rather than upon the lesson itself. These methods have their place, but their place is not that of making the lesson interesting and holding attention. There are many and various methods that may be used to make the lesson more real, to illustrate, to help fix the lesson in definite form. But these methods should involve the use of nothing that does not bear directly and vitally on the lesson. They should direct attention to the lesson rather than to the device used. Otherwise the pupil will remember the device and forget or miss utterly the more vital things we wished him to learn. His interest flags as soon as the exciting story is ended or the "object" laid aside. Steady, quiet, persistent attention and activity are made impossible. There is "oscillation of excitement and apathy," "alternation between periods of overstimulation and inertness." There are developed a dangerous dependence upon external appeals and a morbid appetite for the trivial, the exciting, and the merely pleasurable. "To get attention, but to something other than the fact to be learned or act to be done, is as bad as to have a pupil remember, but remember the wrong answer."

Summary

Attention follows interest. Holding the attention is not a problem for the teacher of an interested

LEARNING AND TEACHING

class. But for emphasis let it be repeated: *The interest, to be worth anything, must be interest in the lesson itself because the pupil feels that it has some relation to his own life.*

Questions

1. Point out facts that show the importance of attention in the teaching process.

2. What is the difference between spontaneous and voluntary attention?

3. Mention some things that may easily contribute to inattention.

4. What objection have you to "making the lesson interesting"?

5. What are some of the fundamental principles in securing real attention?

CHAPTER XIV

TYPES OF TEACHING

CALL to mind several class sessions at which you have been present and ask regarding each one this question, "Just what was the teacher trying to accomplish in the lesson period?" Then consider the following samples of teaching.

Except in very recent years a large part of college teaching consisted of lectures. The professor came to his class prepared to speak at length on a certain topic. Often he wrote out in full what he intended to say and then read this in class. The students were expected to listen and to take notes on the lecture.

As you consider this method recall the method used under the old system of Chinese education. The pupil went to the teacher, turned his back so that he could not possibly see the book, and then recited in a very loud voice and at top speed what he had memorized.

A favorite classroom practice in the public schools in the past has been that of having the pupils repeat many times certain facts to be learned. We have all heard children repeating: "Twice one is two. Twice two is four. Twice three is six."

Contrast this with this type of lesson: The members of the class undertake to find out something of the geography of their immediate locality. They go out singly or by groups; they investigate; they ask

LEARNING AND TEACHING

questions; they make notes; they come back to the classroom and discuss their discoveries.

In each of the four cases cited there is what is called teaching, but the methods differ greatly. The methods may be called giving information, holding an examination, fixing knowledge, conducting an investigation. We shall need to study each of these methods with care.

Giving Information

This teaching method is not confined to the college lecture hall. The Bible class teacher who does all the talking is following the same method. The term "lecture" is usually reserved for the longer, more systematic effort; while the shorter, more informal speech is called "just telling." The principle in each case is the same. The teacher knows something that he thinks the pupil does not know, and he proceeds to tell him.

This method of teaching has been much used and has been severely criticized. It is often said that "telling is not teaching at all." The method has certainly many disadvantages, and it is not surprising that it has become unpopular. In the first place, people forget most of the things that they are told. Furthermore, the lecturer is liable to waste some, perhaps most, of his time telling his students things that they already know. When he does tell something that the students do not know he often omits so many and so important details that they secure a knowledge that is so piecemeal as to be of little value or even to lead them to an entirely wrong

116

TYPES OF TEACHING

conclusion. The further difficulty is often experienced with students who learn by this method that they are unable to use their knowledge. Still another difficulty is that at the end of a course of lectures the students are often little better able to find out things for themselves than they were at the beginning.

That the method is not altogether without value should, however, be easily evident. The man at the information bureau in a railway station spends most of his time telling things, and he succeeds in imparting a vast amount of very useful information. It is further very practically usable knowledge and is put into effect. A man inquires the time of departure of his train. He finds that it is an hour earlier than he had expected. He cancels his trip uptown and gets the train. The clerk might have advised him to wait and see for himself. That would have resulted in a vivid and long-to-be-remembered piece of information, but it would have been rather expensive. The lecture method is quick and economical. A lecturer who knows his topic can tell a large company of people in half an hour things about China or Bolivia or Palestine that they could not discover for themselves in five years of continuous residence in those countries.

Examination

In an effort to make the method of telling more effective teachers have often added oral or written examinations. By this means they have attempted to compel the students to remember the content of

117

LEARNING AND TEACHING

the lecture. In some cases the teachers still make the telling primary and make use of the examination as a check on the effectiveness of the work. In other cases teachers have gone to the opposite extreme and put practically the whole emphasis on the examination. They have found that they could dispense with the telling part by referring the students to text-books and have given over the class period almost entirely to quizzing the pupils on the content of a section of work assigned in advance. This is the type of teaching referred to under the title "Holding an Examination."

The testing takes various forms. The pupil may be required to repeat the whole material in his own words or even rehearse it in exactly the words of the textbook. Another way is to ask a number of more or less random questions distributed in such a way that no member of the class may feel safe unless he knows the whole of the topic of the day. Sometimes the questions are asked orally in the class session; at other times they are put in a written examination.

The old-time Chinese teacher was not the sole practitioner of this method. It has been extensively used everywhere and is indeed perhaps the most widely used school method in existence. It has obvious advantages, but it also has been found to have disadvantages. Students often acquire a facility for predicting what questions will be asked and then prepare for these questions only. Even when they prepare a larger amount of material it is often done by a process of "cramming" that enables the student to

TYPES OF TEACHING

remember the material for a short time and then quite forget most of it later. As a result of this method we sometimes find individuals who graduate from school or college with the highest honors and yet who are able to do only very inferior work in practical life.

Testing has been considerably used, but has not been very satisfactory in Sunday-school work. In week-day school the penalties inflicted on a pupil who has failed to recite satisfactorily are often so unpleasant that he mends his ways. Since in Sunday school we are not able to reward or punish so effectively, the method is less useful.

Drill

When a teacher finds that the pupil does not pay attention to the telling and also finds that the examination is not a sufficiently strong lever to secure the desired results, recourse is sometimes had to another method called "drill." The material to be remembered is compressed to the smallest possible size, and then the class, usually as a whole, is set to work to rehearse the lesson until it is well memorized. Occasionally elaborate devices are used to somewhat lighten the burden of this work. Every one is familiar with the various games and puzzles from which one is expected to secure a knowledge of the alphabet and of the simpler mathematical relations. In other cases no attention is paid to these devices, but the citadel is taken by bold frontal attack.

The method of drill undoubtedly has its place in

119

LEARNING AND TEACHING

our educational practice. It is necessary that we should make certain things as nearly as possible automatic. This is true of many things in general education, and applies to some points in religious education. It is well that we should know in a general way, perhaps exactly, where to find each book in the Bible. There is no particular virtue in having this knowledge except that it makes the Bible more usable. We should memorize perfectly the Lord's Prayer, some great selections of Scripture, and some of our finest hymns. The purpose here, again, is to make them more usable. For instance, if, when engaging in a service of worship where the Lord's Prayer is used, we can repeat it correctly without hesitation, we are then able to give our whole attention to the meaning of what we are saying, whereas if we knew it very imperfectly we would spend most of our energies trying to recall the words.

Investigation

To a degree in all times, but particularly in our own day, teachers have felt that neither by the use of one of these methods alone nor by the use of all together could they secure the educational results that they desired. Having studied the methods by which individuals and groups outside of school learn, they have endeavored to carry over these methods to school work. They have found that the knowledge that is gained from actual experience is the knowledge that is usually retained and is usable. As a result we have introduced laboratories and excursions as a part of our school practice.

120

TYPES OF TEACHING

Some serious difficulties arise, however, in the use of this method. To begin with, it is slow and expensive. The child who learns the meaning of "burn" by touching a red-hot iron will not soon forget it, but will probably pay a high price for his knowledge. Again, it is quite impossible for a student to cover the desired amount of material by this method. With young and inexperienced students it is particularly wasteful. The method is somewhat expedited by the provision of a few fundamental suggestions by the teacher. By watching the pupil's progress and checking his plan of work where it seems likely to lead to entirely unprofitable or to really disastrous results the teacher is able to economize the pupil's time. The pupil gets his knowledge faster with the assistance of a laboratory manual or a supervisor than without one.

In addition to merely gathering data and discovering the simple laws involved, it is, of course, necessary that there should be thought that leads to larger generalizations. This is accomplished by a discussion wherein the teacher endeavors to develop knowledge rather than to provide it. When the class meets after the excursion the teacher does not proceed to lecture the students on the meaning and importance of what they have seen, but, chiefly by means of questions, encourages discussion. This is often called the developmental method. The students are not left entirely to themselves to find out what they can, nor are they dogmatically controlled. They are active, not passive; and the result is thought that is worth while.

LEARNING AND TEACHING

The Sunday-school teacher will be confronted with the problem as to which of these methods he should use. Should he do most of the talking? or should he use the discussion method? Should his chief task be the assignment of home work and the quizzing of the class by questions or by written examinations on the work that they are supposed to do outside the class session? Will he need to use the method of drill? To what extent should he expect his pupils to make a first-hand study of the actual work of the Church both in the local community and in foreign lands?

Relation of Method and Purpose

It will be clear that all of these methods are of value, but that all have their limitations; and unless they are used intelligently, they will hinder rather than further the pupil's progress. The teacher's first task is not to choose his method, but to choose his purpose. He must ask: "What is it that I want to do in this lesson period?" Having his purpose clearly in mind, he can then choose the method to be used to realize his aim. In every lesson one of these methods will be used. It is more probable that two or more of them will be used in combination. The factor which determines the general plan of the lesson period should not be the teacher's admiration for any particular method, but what he or she desires to accomplish in that lesson. If the pupils need to acquire, as a background for their thinking, a fund of information regarding ancient peoples and their customs, it may seem best to use the lecture

TYPES OF TEACHING

method. On the other hand, while the pupils may obtain less information, they may come to understand those peoples better if they themselves search old documents and visit museums. The important point is that the methods, be they one or many, should be selected, not by chance, but with a view to what is to be accomplished.

It will be seen, then, how different methods may be called into play in one lesson. After the pupils have made themselves familiar with the general point of view of the subject which is under consideration, it may seem advisable for the sake of economy of time to resort to the lecture method. A teacher who thus attempts a combination of methods will need to be especially conscious of the aim of his lesson, that each step may be a definite contribution to the whole plan and that the whole be a unity and not a conglomeration.

Questions

1. Give examples of particular class sessions in which the various types of teaching have been used.

2. What advantages would be obtained by the introduction of a system of examinations into our Sunday schools?

3. What disadvantages do you see in a liberal use of examinations?

4. In the teaching of a particular lesson how would you decide as to which method or methods you would use?

CHAPTER XV

STORY-TELLING

Of the scant records that we possess of the life and teaching of Jesus, a considerable part is taken up with accounts of the stories he told. Now, it is quite fair to suppose that the writers of the Gospels in their selection of materials gave prominence to those things that they remembered most clearly and that seemed to be most prominent and valuable in the sayings of Jesus both at the time of utterance and at the time of writing. It is therefore evident that Jesus made a large and effective use of stories and that they were easily remembered.

In this respect Jesus was not unlike other teachers. From earliest times the story has been much used as a means of teaching. Books on primitive life and customs dwell at length on the story and the story-teller. In Oriental life to-day, where certain elements of primitive life have still been preserved, the story-teller is a familiar figure. In the Western World of our own time there has been a marked revival of story-telling; and as a result, in school, library, and social settlement, story-telling has become a fine art.

In modern religious education also the story is being given a large place, but the justification therefor is neither the fact that it is highly commended by educators in other fields nor the fact that it is interesting and attractive to our classes. The real

124

STORY - TELLING

test of its usefulness in our work is the extent to which it contributes to the religious development of our pupils. We must therefore examine the story in the light of what we know about religious development and see the way or ways in which it contributes to that development.

Jesus's Stories

We cannot do better than begin our study with an examination of some of Jesus's stories. Let us see, if we can, how his stories touched and changed the religious life of his hearers. The group of stories in the fifteenth chapter of Luke may be taken as typical. What was the life attitude that Jesus wanted to alter? The situation is clearly shown in the verses preceding: "Now all the publicans and sinners were drawing near unto him to hear him. And both the Pharisees and the scribes murmured, saving, This man receiveth sinners, and eateth with them." (Luke xv. 1, 2.) Then follow Jesus's three stories—one of the finding of the lost sheep, the second regarding the finding of the lost coin, and finally the story of the return of the prodigal son.

The last of the group was particularly pointed. Here was a boy who had been foolish and now was returning with a prayer for forgiveness. The father rejoiced; but the elder brother was spiteful and angry, for his position of solitary favoritism was being affected. The hearers could scarcely fail to be stirred with disgust and anger at the unpardonable selfishness of the elder brother. Think now of the parallel. Here they were, the Pharisees and scribes, the fa-

125

LEARNING AND TEACHING

vored brothers, boasting of their continued faithfulness to God, despising the wayward Gentiles, and angry and resentful when those brothers returned to the family circle.

Jesus might have simply denounced this attitude and have tried to argue them into a better way of thinking, but instead he told this simple story and left them to draw their own conclusions. The story portrayed a certain situation and a certain way of acting in that situation, and the hearers could hardly fail to develop a feeling of dissatisfaction with that way of acting. Argument would probably have produced counter-argument, but to the story there was no reply. He simply narrated facts and left the story to do its own work. Of course the whole group of stories was not enough to break up the deeply-rooted habits that many of them had developed; but this story has been, both then and ever since, a mighty onslaught on snobbishness.

Of all the examples that are preserved to us of Jesus's stories, it is fair to say that every one was chosen to accomplish certain specific things in the situations which he met and that they fitted perfectly those needs. In each case there was a certain principle of living that his hearers were not sufficiently appreciating. The story enabled the hearers to see for themselves the practical outworking of the principles at stake.

The Educational Value of the Story

See how the story relates itself to the ways in which an individual learns. The fisherman finds luck

STORY - TELLING

in a certain place to-day. Unless something else intervenes to hinder him, he will surely return to-morrow to the same spot. Continued luck in one place and continued bad luck in another will soon teach him where to fish. The child cries and is fondled. He cries again when he wants further attention. Jesus fed the multitude, and the next day they sought him again. These are but samples of the working of the law of our learning. We do something, we watch the results, we regard the result as satisfactory or as unsatisfactory, and our experience in the case that is passed guides us in the future. Moreover, we are guided not only by the results of what we do, but by the experience of others. We see other fishermen try certain places repeatedly, but always with poor luck, and we do not waste the time and effort to make even one trial. This is a somewhat less direct, but still very effective, way of learning.

It is just here that the story fits in. It portrays conduct and so enlarges experience. It shows us new or forgotten facts and so affects our judgment. It shows us things so vividly that we feel that we are living through the experiences, and our wills are stirred to action.

The story, then, is valuable for religious education if the changes that it causes in the lives of the hearers contribute to their religious development. This is the primary and only fully satisfactory test of the value of the story for our work. The teacher should choose the stories that will help the pupils at the point where they most need help.

The whole aim to be secured includes three rather

LEARNING AND TEACHING

distinct parts. We may wish to point out to the pupils that a certain thing needs to be done. We tell them a story which shows this need. Perhaps the pupils are already familiar with the need, but can see no way of meeting it. Then our story should embody a way of acting under such circumstances. It should show how the thing can be done. Perhaps they already know the need and know what they ought to do, but are rather indifferent to the task. Then we need a story with plenty of feeling in it, so that they will be spurred to action. Sometimes it is possible to combine two or all three of these aspects in one story, but more often it will be found advisable to secure the total result by a group or series of stories.

The primary test which will be used in selecting a story for religious education will, of course, be its ability to contribute to the aim of the religious educator. But, however carefully the story has been selected from the point of view of the experience portrayed, it cannot accomplish the best results unless the story-teller has mastered the technique of story-telling. The form of the story and the manner of telling it, while of secondary importance, are decidedly important. In the following paragraphs some of the commonly accepted principles of story-telling are mentioned.

The Marks of a Good Story

The story must have plenty of action. Description deals with conditions; the story sets forth activities. Description shows what is; the story tells

STORY - TELLING

what is done. This is perhaps the chief reason for the popularity of the story with children. They have not yet come to take much interest in abstractions and generalizations; they are chiefly interested in what happens. The adult searches for causal forces, and his question is: "Why was that done in that way?" The child cares little for the logic of the matter; his question is: "What happened next?" The story should move quickly, presenting a series of clean-cut pictures. Care should be taken to present enough detail to make it vivid, but not enough to confuse or weary the hearer. It is particularly important that the continuity of the pupil's thought be not broken by the use of words with which he is not familiar.

Some stories possess the serious fault of ending unsatisfactorily. Children make friends with the persons and even the things of the story. They will be quite disturbed if at the end of the story there is suspense and doubt regarding the safety and comfort of those concerned. The hearer's interest and attention will thus be taken away from the point of importance and value.

A further test of a good story is that it should be true to life. This does not mean that fables, myths, and fairy stories should be ruled out. Indeed, they are often wonderfully true to life. It does mean that the story should not give a distorted idea of the principles that underlie our everyday living. The story of the little girl who was so careful of her knitting that she never dropped a stitch and who was taken away on a snow-white horse to live in a king's

9   129

LEARNING AND TEACHING

palace, surrounded with attendants and luxuries for the remainder of her life, is a sample of a common type of story which it not true to life. The little girl who is careful with her work in the hope that she will have some such future will soon be disappointed and probably will decide that it really does not pay to be careful. If the story held up as a reward the satisfaction that comes with work well done, the educational result would be far better.

Not all story-tellers would have stopped where Jesus did in the story of the Good Samaritan. Many would have added that just as the Samaritan was helping the wounded man up he saw a beautiful pearl that the robbers had dropped in their haste. This would have spoiled the story. After all, the joy of being a good neighbor is really worth more than pearls and other similar treasures.

It will be evident, then, that most stories available need to be changed before being used for religious education. Some are in themselves faulty merely as stories, but more often the difficulty arises that they are not adapted to the purpose to be accomplished. Often the story points out something that needs to be done, but the only way suggested of meeting the need is a way that is quite impossible for the particular pupils who are to hear it. Changes will then have to be made so that it will suit this particular situation. The teacher may find that a story used a year ago with another class will not suit at all the class now being taught and that drastic revision is needed.

130

STORY - TELLING

Telling Stories

All this has dealt with the choice of the story. There still remains the very important question of how to tell the story. So much is available on this point in the various books on story-telling that it is only necessary to say a little here. However, the little said must not be taken to imply that the point is of small importance. It is, indeed, of the largest significance. While skill in telling cannot make a poor story good, the lack of it may easily render the best story of little value.

The first task of the story-teller after choosing the story and adapting it to the situation is to become thoroughly familiar with it. It is not necessary to memorize it verbatim except in places where there is repetition of a phrase and the exact wording is therefore of importance. Indeed, there are disadvantages in memorizing the whole story.

The story must be appreciated and enjoyed by the story-teller. If you are ashamed of a story, do not tell it. If you have a really worth-while story, tell it with confidence and enthusiasm. The narrative should not be allowed to drag, but the fault is more often that the story is told too rapidly. The words should be given slowly enough for the hearers to get them clearly.

Sometimes the story-teller omits an important point of the story. It is generally unwise to go back to make the connection, for this breaks the continuity of the hearer's thought and spoils the story.

Finally, having told the story, do not add an application. It may be wise to ask some questions that

131

LEARNING AND TEACHING

will stimulate the hearers to think and to form opinions and resolutions, but these judgments to be of value must be theirs and not yours. If the story has not set forth experience sufficiently clearly that they may come to a decision, the teacher's advice will not be welcome. If they have seen the point, the advice will not be needed and will probably be resented. Attention to these rules may at first seem to be a hindrance rather than a help. However, after a little persistent practice the story-teller will find that the success attained will amply repay for the labor involved.

Questions

1. Read again the story of the Good Samaritan with the verses that come before and after. (Luke x. 25-37.) What purpose did Jesus seem to have in telling this story?

2. What advantages has the story over "merely telling"?

3. What are the marks of a good story?

4. What are some of the most important rules for the telling of a story?

CHAPTER XVI

USING ILLUSTRATIONS

THERE are three classes of illustrations commonly used in religious education—objects, pictures, and incidents. Objects and pictures are used principally with younger pupils and incidents with older ones, but this distinction is not rigidly adhered to. Most teachers agree that the lesson that is without illustration is almost certainly destined to be dull and that good illustrations are a guarantee of an attentive and interested class.

It is quite to be expected that some illustrations will be more useful than others and that the illustration that is excellent in one lesson will not be the best in another. What illustrations are good and how and when to use them is not to be learned by the memorizing of a few rules. We must study the problem with sufficient care to understand the underlying principles of the use of illustrations. This will enable us to choose our illustrations intelligently and to use them skillfully.

The Use of Objects

For the custom of using objects in the work of teaching we are greatly indebted to a Swiss teacher named Heinrich Pestalozzi. When he began his work, about one hundred and fifty years ago, teaching was chiefly a means of getting the pupils to memorize the contents of books. Pestalozzi said

LEARNING AND TEACHING

that things rather than books should be studied, and he introduced object talks into his class work. He was not the only educational reformer who advocated this point of view, but he, perhaps more than any one else, made "object talks" popular.

To most of Pestalozzi's theory in this matter we must give ready approval. The person who has never seen a banana can gain a better knowledge of it in three minutes by looking at it, by feeling it, and by tasting it than he could get in a much longer time by hearing some one talk about it. As an elaboration of this principle teachers to-day are making extensive use of laboratories, museums, and excursions. When the class is studying Roman history the pupils are taken to the museum, where they can see for themselves bowls and vases and other articles that have been preserved from Roman times and which help them to understand Roman life and customs. When the study deals with the production of cotton and the manufacture of it into cloth, the pupils are taken to see a cotton mill, if one is within reach, and the result is a great increase in their knowledge of how cloth is made.

When we come to examine the use of object teaching in religious education, we have to ask what it is that we want to make clear. There may come to mind the thought of ancient Hebrew tents and of the hills and valleys of Palestine. Certainly models and relief maps contribute decidedly to clearing up our ideas on these points. It must be remembered, however, that knowing the geography of Palestine and the size and shape of a phylactery is not the ulti-

USING ILLUSTRATIONS

mate end of our work. We seek changed lives; we wish the members of our classes to love God and their neighbors, and the knowledge of the geography of Palestine is valuable religiously only in so far as it contributes to this Christian ideal of living.

Missionary object lessons are also in much favor. Here the knowledge of the construction of Chinese houses or the method of dressing African babies is valuable, but its value lies in its contribution to a better feeling on the part of the pupils toward the Chinese and African peoples. If the pupils at the end of the lesson feel that these peoples are foolish and degraded, the lesson has not been helpful. If they are brought to see in these peoples worthy fellow members of the family of God, possessing many excellent characteristics, but in need of certain things we can give them, then the lesson has been really missionary.

Symbolism

Objects are often used in a symbolic sense. A piece of moth-eaten cloth is exhibited to show how sin destroys life. A drop of chemical is put into a glass of colored water to clear it and to show how the power of God can cleanse a soiled life. A magnet is used to lift pieces of iron, showing how God can draw people to himself. These and similar devices are much used for illustrating talks to children.

This symbolic use of objects is of doubtful value, especially with children. Of course the objects catch the attention of the young people, but almost invariably the interest is in the exhibition and not in the moral application. This type of teaching is common-

LEARNING AND TEACHING

ly supposed to be much more suited for work with children than for work with adults. As a matter of fact, the opposite is more nearly correct. Adults may find the symbolism far-fetched, but to the child, who is little given to symbolism and abstraction, the parallel is not in evidence at all. The child's interest in the object sermon is chiefly because of the fireworks and not because of an appreciation of the underlying teaching.

At this point mention should be made of the use of blackboard designs, for this method also is based on the idea of symbolism. Many of them are fearfully and wonderfully made, but are of slight educational value. Here, again, the adult beholds them with rather small interest, but considers that "they are fine for children." As a matter of fact, they are distinctly an adult creation and are of little value to the child.

Pictures and Drawing

The second main class of illustrations includes pictures and drawings. These are extensively used in Sunday school and offer wide possibilities of usefulness. To the child who has never seen a sheep or a shepherd the story of the good shepherd yields little meaning. The best plan would be to bring the child to see a shepherd and flock of sheep; but since that is almost always impossible, the next best method is to show pictures. The teacher should always remember, however, that merely showing pretty pictures which the children will enjoy is not enough. The picture, in order to make a real contribution to the lesson, must help to make more real to the pupils

USING ILLUSTRATIONS

the situation or the people which the lesson aims to present to them. Thus their impression of that situation will be more vivid and lasting, and the religious development of the class will be furthered.

Drawings and diagrams are also of value in making clear the points under consideration. Lack of artistic ability should not prevent the teacher's use of this method. The diagram should be reasonably neat and accurate, but the emphasis should not be on the mechanical skill involved. The real test of the value of such illustrations is the extent to which they make clear to the pupils the point under discussion.

Anecdotes

Finally, we must consider the third main class, the incident or anecdote used for illustrative purposes. Sometimes these brief stories are used as a means of catching the interest. Teachers often begin the lesson with a story of the baseball field or of the week's happenings or with some tale of adventure. They then endeavor to make the transition to the lesson so quickly that the pupils are swept along in spite of themselves. Used in this way, illustrations have the disadvantage that if they are not rather thrilling they do not usually get the attention at all; and if they are successful in this respect, they get it so thoroughly that it is impossible to take the pupil's mind off them and fix it on the lesson.

A better plan in the use of the story is to make it not a bait or a sugar coating, but a part of the lesson itself. An abstract discussion of the joy of service or the glory of self-forgetfulness or the beauty

LEARNING AND TEACHING

of honesty and humility or the fact that Christianity is essentially a missionary religion in origin, in development, and in outlook will probably be of little interest or value to a class of young children. If the class discussion deals with practical activities in each of these respects, the work will be much more likely to be interesting and profitable. Younger people find more need for illustrations than do older ones, for they have not yet accumulated so large a body of experience, and experience is a necessary basis for thought and discussion.

The Final Test

The illustration, then, is valuable to the extent that it really contributes to the attainment of our final aim. If by means of object, picture, or anecdote the pupil's experience is enlarged and his thinking helped and this thinking is in the direction of a fuller religious life, the use of the illustration is justifiable. If it supplies facts that are irrelevant, or if it distracts the thinking, then it is a nuisance rather than a help. Illustrations are not only advisable, but are indispensable to the learning process; but their business is to supply the concrete experiences needed to enable the individual to form the judgments and resolutions necessary for the regulation of his life.

Questions

1. If you were teaching a class of fourteen-year-old boys, would you need a blackboard? Just what use would you make of it?

2. Examine the pictures provided with the Graded Les-

USING ILLUSTRATIONS

son course for Beginners. What is the purpose of the use of these pictures in this course?

3. What use would you make of missionary curios in a Sunday school?

4. How would you distinguish between the story as a "bait" and as a real part of the lesson itself?

CHAPTER XVII

ASKING QUESTIONS

SKILL in asking questions is commonly considered to be a primary qualification for good teaching. Teachers are incessantly urged to lecture less and question more. They are told that Socrates was the great questioner and that all good teachers follow his example. We can therefore well afford to study in some detail the matter of questioning.

Types of Questions

A comparison of school questions with questions in out-of-school life shows an interesting point of difference. Ordinarily, when one individual asks another a question he is endeavoring to get some information that he thinks the other person may be able to give. The question in everyday life is essentially a method of getting information.

The question in school is usually of a quite different nature. Occasionally the teacher may ask the pupils the reason for their lateness or absence. In such a case the purpose is to secure information not already possessed. But this type of question is not what is usually meant when teachers are advised to ask questions. The teacher does not ask the pupil a question in order to get information, for he already possesses more information on the topic than does the student. The question in school is usually asked with the purpose of measuring the pupil's

ASKING QUESTIONS.

knowledge. The purposes involved in the school question and in the out-of-school question are about as far removed from each other as is possible.

There is another type of question which has a place in school work and which has recently received a greater emphasis than formerly. This type of question is designed primarily to develop the knowledge of the pupil. When Jesus told the story of the good Samaritan he concluded by asking the question, "Which of these three, thinkest thou, proved neighbor unto him that fell among the robbers?" Evidently this question was not asked merely for information nor as a test, but to drive those of whom it was asked to further and clearer thinking.

There are, then, three main classes of questions— those asked simply for information, those asked to test knowledge, and those asked to stimulate thinking. While this classification is useful, it should be stated that the three cannot be sharply separated. The question asked mainly for the purpose of testing knowledge may also assist in its development. The question asked to encourage thinking may well reveal the pupil's present knowledge. The question for information may accomplish both of the other purposes in addition to its own.

The Purpose of the Question

The type of question used will depend largely on the teacher's conception of his task. If the teacher believes that his first task is to assign lessons and see that they are memorized, he will probably confine himself chiefly to the test question. If he considers

141

LEARNING AND TEACHING

that the main task is not so much the discovery of the pupil's range of knowledge or diligence of preparation, but rather the development of that knowledge, he will probably emphasize the question that prods he pupil's thinking.

The first-mentioned, informational type of question is also coming to have an emphasis in school work. This is the result of the democratic tendency in the schoolroom which tends to regard the school as an institution where a group of students are working together. Within this group there are more experienced students called teachers, and there are less experienced students called pupils; but they are all facing common problems on which none have full information.

A good example of this type of work is found in the class session, where the task is the planning of a program of Christian activity for the class. There is some money in the class treasury and more coming in. There are many ways in which the money might be spent. The class spends some time in discussing and planning the best ways of spending that money. One member of the class has been reading during the week of the needs of a mission school in Syria. Another pupil feels that something should be done for a certain family of which the breadwinner has been suddenly thrown out of work. Another believes that this particular sum of money should go to the denominational missionary board. The teacher has ideas also, but does not know just how urgent are the needs of the family mentioned and has not read the account of this piece of mission work in Syria.

ASKING QUESTIONS

No member of the class is therefore ready to cast his vote. Before making a decision the class spends some time in consideration of the various projects. Under such circumstances as these the questions asked will be primarily for the sake of getting information. Many teachers believe that in most cases this type of study is the most fruitful and economical method of work. They further hold that the informational question really tests and develops thought better than the question specifically prepared for those purposes.

The teacher's first task is to examine carefully the reasons for asking questions and then to frame the questions with these purposes clearly in mind. While this involves hard work, it is essential to the best teaching.

The Characteristics of a Good Question

A few practical suggestions may be given as to the characteristics of good questions.

The question should be clear. It would be absurd to ask a six-year-old child, "What is your deliberate estimation of the ethical quality of the Hebrew patriarch's ultimate solution of the unfortunate conflict between his nephew's insistent demands and his own vested interests?" But it might be quite advisable to ask, "What do you think of Abraham's way of ending the quarrel between Lot and himself?" In the first case the pupil's entire energy would have to be given to untangling the question, whereas he should be giving himself to solving the problem. This case is extreme, but examination of the ques-

LEARNING AND TEACHING

tions asked in school shows that in many cases the phrasing is not readily intelligible to the pupils.

The question should provoke thought, not confusion. It should encourage thinking rather than guessing. A teacher asked a senior class the question, "What is salt?" and wondered why the students gave no answer. The questions should be such that the pupils are spurred to think and to think in the direction of the solution of the main problem in hand.

The "elliptical" question is especially liable to be confusing. "If I were in a room where the air was bad, I would ——?" might bring the answers: "Not like it;" "feel unwell;" "not do as good work;" "open the window;" "leave the room." Indeed, the list of things that I might do is almost endless. When such a question as this is asked, the pupil usually tries to guess what the teacher wants. This may serve as a mental gymnastic, but that is not the teacher's purpose. If the question were put, "What effect has bad air upon health?" the results would be more satisfactory.

The question should not be too easy. Many teachers ask long lists of questions, all of which can be answered without a moment's hesitation. It is often said that questions that can be answered with "Yes" or "No" should not be asked. This is an overstatement, for some "Yes" and "No" questions involve much thinking. Jesus asked the question, "Are ye able to drink of the cup that I drink of?" The answer to be expected would be "Yes" or "No," but to get that answer there was necessary an intensity of

144

ASKING QUESTIONS

thinking that could not but have important results. The test of the question, then, should be, not the possibility of answering it by "Yes" or "No," but the probable amount of thought that it inspires.

The question should not suggest the answer. Of this group of questions, Is God good? Does God love us? Ought we to love God? there is not one that tends to provoke real thinking. The asking of such questions as these tends to encourage guessing or merely verbal answers. There is but slight educational value in such a process.

There is also the possibility of making the questions too difficult. Frequently teachers ask questions that require for their answers a range of knowledge and experience quite beyond the possibilities of the pupils.

How to Ask Questions

It is important that the questions should interest the whole class and be so distributed that all members of the class will be busy all of the time. If the questions are asked of only a small group, or if they are asked in rotation, there may be developed a tendency to attend to the topic in hand only when the question is in immediate proximity. For the same reason it is advised that such a question as, "John, what is a Pharisee?" should be worded, "What is a Pharisee, John?" Calling on the individual and then asking the question may develop the habit of inattention. Knowing that the name will come last and that the question will not be repeated leaves the pupil no choice but to be continually on the watch.

LEARNING AND TEACHING

A commonly accepted rule is that the teacher should not repeat the question or the answer. Mechanically followed, this rule may prove a hindrance to the best work, but in the main it is good. There are two objections to repeating questions and answers—it wastes time, and it encourages inattention by leading the pupils to feel that continuous attention is not necessary.

Teachers are commonly advised to prepare carefully a small number of "pivotal" questions and then to fit in others as the particular situation demands. To prepare all of the questions in advance would not only be an enormous task, but would render the class work mechanical and lifeless.

It is well that the teacher should, wherever possible, approve the answers given by the pupil. This is particularly important if the pupil is inclined to be timid and hesitant about participating in the work. The teacher's attitude toward the pupil should not humiliate nor discourage him. This does not mean that incorrect conclusions should go unchallenged or uncorrected, but that the teacher should utilize the better aspects of the answer and by developing the right rather than by combating the wrong should lead to correct thinking.

Frequently the "wrong" answer is the result of a badly phrased question. Many so-called "wrong" answers are not really wrong, but are not the aspects of the matter that are needed in the discussion of the moment. It is a good plan not only to prepare the questions, but to think of the various answers that may be expected to be given to them. The teacher

146

ASKING QUESTIONS

may also profit by sitting down after the lesson to a study of the answers given by the pupils and to a consideration of the reasons for incorrect or unexpected answers. Are they usually the result of inadequate or incorrect knowledge on the part of the pupils or of clumsy phrasing of the question by the teacher?

Pupils' Questions

Another point of great importance is the matter of pupils' questions. Occasionally a teacher is found who is quite nettled when pupils persist in asking questions. The folly of such an attitude is too obvious to require discussion. Indeed, some educators would go so far as to measure the value of the teacher's work by the number and the quality of the questions asked by the pupils.

Attention to rules is in the main helpful, but is not by itself a guarantee of successful class work. The really indispensable mark of a good question is that it be concise and clear and turn the energy of the pupils to getting the right answer by thinking and not by guessing. The more thoroughly the class work is a vital and genuinely coöperative discussion of real problems, the less need will there be for attention to rules.

Questions

1. What is the difference between the type of question commonly used in the schoolroom and the question as used in ordinary life?

2. Which of these two kinds of questions is the best stimulant to thinking?

LEARNING AND TEACHING

3. Show how the question as used in out-of-school life may be used also in the classroom.

4. Mention some of the characteristics of a good question.

5. How much value would you attach to pupils' questions?

CHAPTER XVIII

ACTIVITY IN LEARNING AND LIVING

MORE than once in preceding chapters we have urged the importance of the teacher's seeing to it that the pupil has opportunities to act upon the lessons that he is taught, that his impulses be allowed actually to issue in good deeds. "No impression without expression" is a familiar pedagogical maxim. The necessity of enlisting the activity of the pupil in learning in the Sunday school is coming more and more to be insisted upon. Systems of "expressional activities" are being elaborated for the various grades and their importance urged upon Sunday-school workers. We shall wish to see why they are essential elements in the learning process.

Let us recognize, first and fundamentally, that it is active Christians that we desire as the result of the learning process. If it were not so, activity in learning would not be so vitally necessary. Other methods might suffice. If accurate memory for facts and doctrines and if emotional experiences were alone to satisfy us, we would need to attach little importance to activity in learning because activity in living would be unimportant. But the Church needs the Christian who lives what he knows and what he feels, who translates creeds into service and whose emotional promptings do not evaporate, but embody themselves into concrete deeds. Activity is important in learning, because it is important

149

LEARNING AND TEACHING

in living. Only through activity in learning can the right kind of activity in living be assured.

The Psychological Basis

Let us see why this last statement is true by considering what might happen in a particular case of learning. A boy hears a story that arouses in him an impulse to kind ideas. What may happen? In the first place, it is conceivable that he may never encounter a situation in which he could perform a kind act. The "impression" made by the story and the impulses generated would then, to say the least, be useless. But this is unlikely. Let us suppose that he does encounter a situation in which a kind deed can be done and that he fails to do it, either because there are stronger motives in another direction or because it has been so long since the impression was made that it has lost the impulsive power which it had at first. The impression in this case has been worse than useless. It has been positively harmful. For each occurrence of this sort means that the habit is being definitely established of allowing evil or lower impulses to overcome good ones, or of allowing good impulses to lead nowhere. This means in the one case the development of callousness and indifference in the end or, in the other case, the sentimentalism that revels in emotional experiences and never does anything.

But suppose this boy goes from the story in the fine glow of feeling that it arouses and, yielding to his impulses, actually does something that embodies the lesson of the story and that expresses the feel-

150

ACTIVITY IN LEARNING AND LIVING

ings he experiences. Here the fundamental laws of learning will insure that there is being established, each time this happens, the habit of doing helpful things under the sway of altruistic feeling and impulse. The doing of each good deed increases the chance of good deeds becoming habitual.

In short, whatever the feeling or impulse aroused by a situation, the response is not complete until the impulse issues in action, until feeling determines conduct. The action may be, of necessity often is, deferred. But psychology tells us that "all consciousness is motor"—that is, that every idea tends to issue in action. It is only by having the process completed in action that as teachers we can be certain as to what kind of conduct the experiences we give our pupils will lead to. It is right conduct that we wish to insure. And it can be insured only by making conduct a part of the learning process. That situations shall call forth right responses in the future we must see to it that they call forth right responses *now*.

It should be very clear from what has been said that the "expressional activity" that genuinely completes the learning process is the spontaneous issuing into action of the impulses started by the new forms of experience. It is not just any sort of activity. The teacher should clearly understand this and not be led to feel that just because his pupils are kept doing something with their hands he is realizing the highest educational possibilities. To arouse an impulse to help others and then to set the child to cutting out and pasting pictures is not to

151

LEARNING AND TEACHING

furnish means of expression for the impression made. To let the boy model the walls of Jericho is not to satisfy the impulses aroused in him by the stirring tales of the conquest of Canaan. These activities may be useful, but not as "expression" of the "impression." Manual methods, dramatization, and so on are valuable agencies in education. But what they do is to contribute new forms of experience. Muscular and tactile sensations are added to those from eye and ear. This helps to clarify the experience. Further, the interest is increased because the imitative and constructive tendencies are enlisted. These added forms of experience and this added interest serve to deepen and extend the whole "impression." But they do not "express" it. Genuine expression of the vital sort can come only in the experiences and problems of the child's own life where he has opportunity to act in line with the impulses that the new experience has aroused.

Educational Corollaries

The teacher, then, should provide opportunities for such genuine expression of impressions made, for action upon good impulses aroused, that fine feelings are stirred. Until this is done learning is incomplete. Choices should be made to issue in action. What is not expressed dies. And what is even more serious is the fact that the passive reception of ideas and the excitation of emotions that do not find expression in action tend to develop the habit of inactivity and in James's phrase an "inertly sentimental condition" fatal in the end to will power and to

152

ACTIVITY IN LEARNING AND LIVING

character. "We need in the Sunday school especially to watch," writes Dr. Cope, "lest the spiritual life of the young people be early suffocated with emotion unexpressed in action, feelings that have never wrought out through the muscles, and ideals that have remained unexpressed."

Cope writes further, in his "Efficiency in the Sunday School": "Most of all, we ought to be looking for things for the people in our Sunday schools to be doing. The school must become a laboratory. Virtues must be learned through their practice. We do need graded lessons; but, verily, we need still more what might be called 'going' lessons, so practical that pupils are impelled to practice them, while the school is compelled to direct the practice and open up opportunities for it."

Again: "The most difficult problem before the Sunday school to-day lies right here: How can we find suitable expressional things for our people to do? In fact, the problem goes all through the life of the Church and the whole work of religious education. We are coming into a fairly clear place as to the lesson material for religious education. We are still in the dark as to what is really of greater importance, the opportunities for service, for activities which are the means by which we learn and through which we express, and so make permanent that which is learned."[1]

It is by actual experience in service, apprenticeship training in Christian living that efficient Christian service in maturity can be insured. The prac-

[1] Pages 161-164.

LEARNING AND TEACHING

tice trip on which Jesus sent the disciples illustrates the great Teacher's method of training for service. Significant too in a different way is the conversation with Peter recorded in John xxi. 15-18: "Simon, son of John, lovest thou me? . . . Thou knowest that I love thee. . . . Feed my sheep." The test of character is conduct. And character that measures up to this test is character that has been formed through conduct.

The Will

It should be clear that this habit of acting on impulses and emotional promptings, of expressing choices in decisive action, is the essential thing in "training the will." The will can be trained. How? By training the man, by building character. This is the clear teaching of psychology: the will is the whole man *active*. The man of strong will is the man whose knowledge and experience are rich and full and subject to recall when needed, who can keep his attention centered upon worthy things, however strong the pull of other things, and who, having made his choice in the light of all the knowledge he possesses, is able to act promptly and decisively. The teacher may be sure, then, that all his teaching, in so far as it is good teaching, is developing "will power" in his pupils. If he is supplying them with right ideas, well organized, usable because they have been used, effective because they have been made to issue in action, if he is establishing worthy interests and centering the affections upon right things, he is building character and in so far is training the will. The highest character is that character that is cen-

154

ACTIVITY IN LEARNING AND LIVING

tered in Christ, the Christ life as a pattern determining ideals and principles, the Christ spirit furnishing the motives that determine action, the will of Christ controlling the will of the Christ disciple because the surrendered life means the surrendered will.

Questions

1. How do you account for the fact that to learn to tie the various kinds of rope knots it is necessary not only to be shown how, but also to actually tie the knots?

2. Of how much importance to education is this principle of learning by doing?

3. Point out some ways in which religious education might well make larger use of this principle.

CHAPTER XIX

LEARNING THROUGH DOING

Of the group of questions that we are now studying, that of how to utilize the pupil's activity is perhaps the most important and the most neglected. Whereas the pupil's chief interest is in doing things, the teacher gives him but slight chance to do anything. The pupil is expected to "be quiet and listen," to "speak when spoken to," and to "remember what he has been taught." There is a consequent conflict between the pupil's wish and the teacher's will, and the question of "how to keep order" becomes a real problem.

We may as well admit that the pupil's desire for activity is practically irrepressible. The child who is ready to sit still and listen for long periods of time is usually abnormal in some respect and is probably in need of the help of a physician. Abounding energy working itself out in muscular activities is one of nature's chief endowments to the child. It is as unwise as it is difficult to repress it. The teacher should rather try to develop and at the same time guide it into useful activities.

We must distinguish carefully between merely giving the pupils something to do and using their activities for educational ends. There is undoubtedly some truth in the adage, "Satan finds some mischief still for idle hands to do"; but really to justify the use of activities in religious education we must

156

LEARNING THROUGH DOING

show that they accomplish something beyond merely "killing time." The "thing to do" must make a positive contribution to the teacher's ultimate aim or lose its right to a place in the program.

Handwork in Religious Education

Among the classroom practices designed especially to harness up pupil energy with the accomplishment of educational purposes handwork holds a prominent place. This includes the coloring of outlines, the pasting of pictures, paper-tearing and cutting, drawing, modeling, the making of maps, and notebook work.

Before studying any of these methods in detail it will be well to consider what use we as religious teachers may expect to make of handwork. It has sometimes been argued that manual work is of itself a character-making factor. This, however, is not well supported by evidence. It is not clear that manual workers as a class are of higher moral standards than are brain workers. That physiological conditions have an effect upon moral character is probably beyond dispute, but the validity of that statement is not in itself a sufficient justification for devoting a good share of the Sunday-school period to manual labor.

Nor can we be satisfied with the requirement of mechanical skill as the justification for the use of handwork in religious education. Training in neatness and accuracy is very desirable, provided it be turned into the right channels, but skillfulness of itself does not assure moral character. As a matter

157

LEARNING AND TEACHING

of fact, the professional criminal often manifests a degree of skill that is the despair of those who are charged with the protection of the rights of society. The chief concern of the religious educator is not the development of skill, but rather the control of skill and other possessions by high moral standards. Regarding each class activity, the teacher should ask this question, "Does it contribute to the religious growth of the pupils?"

Drawing

But there are results other than the acquirement of neatness and mechanical skill that handwork may be expected to accomplish and which do justify its inclusion in a program of religious education. For instance, a primary teacher who has told the story of the finding of the baby Moses may suggest to the pupils that they draw pictures illustrating the story. The making of these pictures will serve as an excellent review of the story period. The children will be compelled to rethink the story, filling in gaps, sorting out and organizing the more important items, and making their impressions of the whole story vivid and permanent. In this case and, it will appear later, in others also the value of the handwork lies in the stimulation to clear thinking on the topic under discussion.

Original drawing is a particularly valuable type of handwork, because it can scarcely be done without a considerable amount of independent thinking. The filling in of outlines or the tracing of pictures will probably produce more accurate and artistic results,

LEARNING THROUGH DOING

but the opportunity for originality of thought will be much reduced and the educational effects consequently lessened. The mounting of copies of some of the pictures of our greatest artists has the special value of teaching appreciation of the messages of these masterpieces, but particular care should be taken that this appreciation is really developed and that the work does not become merely mechanical. Selecting the picture to be pasted gives more opportunity for thought than does the pasting. The teacher should, therefore, if possible, have the pupils themselves select the pictures. Even then picture-pasting should not be allowed wholly to replace original work done by the pupils.

In Chapter I. mention was made of a case in which the pupils made drawings to illustrate the topic of the lesson. This handwork not only reviewed the story, but compelled the pupils to take the further step of thinking of various possible ways of carrying out the principle in daily living.

Coloring and Modeling

The coloring of outlines already prepared has perhaps more value in producing thought, but less value in the development of artistic appreciation. Like paper-cutting and tearing, it involves a considerable amount of attention to the mechanical aspects of the work.

Modeling also finds a place in some Sunday schools, but the amount of work and expense involved has limited its use. The simpler, less expensive types undoubtedly are of value. If, when studying

159

LEARNING AND TEACHING

conditions in a mission land, the pupil makes a model of the kind of house used there, he will probably realize its deficiencies more vividly than if he had merely heard about it or looked at pictures of it. Making a relief map will make decidedly vivid the physical features of the country under discussion.

Notebook Work

Another pupil activity that may be included under handwork is notebook work. The pupils may make notes in their own books, or all of the members of the class may contribute toward a single class book. These notes have the value of preserving in brief and convenient form the results of the studies, but they are even more valuable for the thinking that is required to produce them. To put down in a few sentences the gist of the discussion demands a clearness and an organization of thought that is of great value. Sometimes the teacher supplies the brief statement that is to be inserted in the notebooks. In this case much of the value is lost. The summary to be of use must be the result of the pupil's own thinking. This method is particularly valuable with older pupils.

Dramatization

There are certain other types of class work which are closely allied to handwork in the ultimate educational ends secured. Of these, dramatization is particularly popular. Children's love of play is used for educational ends by allowing the pupils to "play" the story they have just heard. Just what happens in such a case? At least it must be admitted that

160

LEARNING THROUGH DOING

the pupils are compelled to think the story through again. They are not only under the necessity of thinking of the various items of the story, but they are compelled to think of the relative importance of these items.

It is sometimes maintained that the child by acting the part of a character actually becomes like that character, that by playing the villain he becomes a villain, and that by playing the good Samaritan he really becomes a good Samaritan. There is, however, no evidence that such a transfer of character takes place, and it is unwise to use dramatization in expectation of such results. Dramatization undoubtedly has an effect on character; but the effect is not produced by transferring the nature of the character to the impersonator, but indirectly by making the story more effective.

Retelling the story or the important points of a previous study is another means of reviewing the work. It is more economical of time and effort than most of the other forms of activity, but is perhaps not so certain to develop a really thorough review.

In all of these activities the relation of expense both in time and money to the results secured should be kept constantly in mind. The value of the work lies, not chiefly in the market value of the material product, but in the educational effect upon the worker. In handwork the inexpensive materials are, in fact, usually more satisfactory from the educational point of view than are expensive ones. The elaborate materials enable the pupils to get results that satisfy them without much thinking, while the cheaper,

LEARNING AND TEACHING

cruder materials make thought and work more necessary. The real value in every case will be in the intelligent appreciation of the subject of study.

A Social Motive

So far we have been speaking only of the cases where the activities are carried on spontaneously for the joy of doing. It is quite possible that in many cases the pupils may have a deeper motive, the giving of pleasure to some one else. The pictures or models may be made for a member of the class not able to be present or for children in the hospital or as a decoration for the classroom or school. The social motive here developed is of the highest importance. The pupils not only receive a stimulus to thought, but are given an opportunity to really do something for others.

In the case of retelling the story a social motive is practically essential. "What was our last Sunday's lesson about?" is almost certain to stimulate little interest and to bring an unsatisfactory reply. If it were put thus, "John and Agnes were ill last week and were not able to be with us; will some one tell them the story?" there would probably be rivalry as to who should have the privilege.

A social motive is necessary in dramatization with older pupils. Young children play the stories just for the fun of it, but older pupils think it "silly." They will respond gladly to the opportunity to play the story for an audience.

In activities where the combined effort of a number of pupils is involved there is an important train-

162

LEARNING THROUGH DOING

ing in social living. As in games and in committee work, so in dramatization the pupils soon discover that it is only by a real coöperation that the undertaking can be made a success. For this reason there should be activities in which all members of the class participate and some in which the whole school unites for a common purpose.

In any class work in which pupils take part care should be taken that it does not tend chiefly to develop self-display and selfish pride. A pupil may retell the story "to show what he knows." He may work hard at handwork to be able to "down" the other fellow. This is about as undesirable a result as could be imagined. Competition is a powerful driving force; but if it destroys the spirit of coöperation and good will, its result is harmful. We certainly do not wish to develop selfish conceit. The introduction of the social motive, the doing of things for others, both crowd out the selfish aspect and work toward the building up of the unselfish attitude.

Apprenticeship in Christian Living

So far we have been speaking of pupil activity as a means by which impressions may be intensified and thinking promoted. When the teacher encourages clay-modeling it is not with the end in view that the pupil shall become an expert pottery maker, but that he shall obtain some quite different abilities. The modeling may be meant to develop such a knowledge and appreciation of Hindu children and their ways of living as will lead to thoroughly Christian attitudes toward them. There is, however, another

LEARNING AND TEACHING

quite different sense in which the pupil may learn by doing. The public school teacher may encourage the pupil to "play grocery" in order that he may thereby improve his knowledge of arithmetic; but the grocer's apprentice is there primarily to learn the grocery business, and no amount of plays and games can take the place of this apprenticeship. Similarly, no one can become an expert teacher without having actually taught, nor can one become a singer without having sung.

What is true of general education is also true of religious education. Here, as elsewhere, doing is the best method of learning. Learning by doing, in the sense of apprenticeship, is to be clearly distinguished from activities that are merely educational methods. Dramatization and clay-modeling are valuable, but not indispensable. There is no substitute for actual Christian living.

At this point the method of Jesus is particularly suggestive. So far as we have any record, Jesus made no use of such things as map-drawing or picture-pasting, but he did make prominent the idea of apprenticeship. The fact that he did not use these school methods does not prohibit our use of them, but it does suggest that it is possible to teach religion without them. The prominence of practice work in his teaching method indicates that it is fundamental.

If religious education to-day were to give to this method the same prominence that Jesus gave it, our whole plan of work would be radically changed. At present we spend most of our time getting pupils to know. We teach them the geography of Palestine

LEARNING THROUGH DOING

and of mission lands. We insist that they shall know Old Testament history and New Testament history and the history of the Christian Church. We organize mission study classes in order that they may know the life and customs of people in non-Christian lands. The emphasis is not so much on doing as on knowing. If we followed the method of Jesus, we would reverse the emphasis. He was primarily interested in what the disciples could do and actually did. True, he instructed them; he held conferences with them; he demonstrated. But all of these were means to an end, that they might be able to do.

It is largely in harmony with this point of view that we have to-day the prominence in Sunday-school work of missionary and other social activities. Social service comes in, therefore, not to crowd out "the lesson," but to give it meaning and usefulness. The very best lesson is the consideration of practical needs which the members of the class as individuals or as a group can supply.

Questions

1. Just what value for religious education do you see in handwork?

2. Which kinds of handwork yield the largest educational results?

3. Which kinds of handwork are especially useful with very young pupils?

4. How may dramatization be used to advantage in the Sunday school?

5. How would you make use of "the social motive" in Sunday-school work?

6. Show how educational results may be secured by having the pupils actually participate in Christian service.

CHAPTER XX

THE TEACHER'S LESSON PLANS

THAT all successful work demands careful planning is so obvious that it scarcely needs restatement. Whether it is the building of a house or an aëroplane or the making of a dress or the preparation of a picnic lunch, the person who does not spend some time in planning the affair will at least be burdened with unnecessary labor and expense and may make a complete failure of the task. In each case there is need for a clear idea of what is to be done and a well-thought-out plan of procedure.

The Need of Planning

The religious teacher also needs careful plans. His task is both difficult and important and calls for the highest skill that he can acquire. He is working for changes in the lives of the pupils. He hopes that these changes will be in the direction of more thoroughly Christian living. Such changes do not simply happen. Without careful planning of the lesson the teacher is likely to overcrowd the time with a multitude of things that are attractive and probably valuable, but which do not contribute in the most direct and fruitful way to the final aim. Only by careful foresight can the teacher make the best use of time and effort and proceed economically to the goal desired.

In this matter the example of Jesus is particularly

THE TEACHER'S LESSON PLANS

helpful. He planned earnestly and carefully. Again and again he withdrew to the solitude to pray and also to plan. Indeed, his praying and his planning were really one. He prayed over his plans, and his plans came out of his prayers. When his work was challenged he was not disturbed; for he knew his final purposes, and he had methodically set out to secure them. His words to Pilate, "To this end came I into the world, that I should bear witness unto the truth," show the support that his plans gave him in the crises of life.

The first essential in good planning is a clear conception of the aim to be attained. This will control the type of plan formulated. It will also serve as a test of the value of each step in the process. We readily admit that the purpose of Sunday-school work is the formation of Christian character, but this statement of aim is not sufficiently specific. We should go farther and show what this involves. We need to determine the aim for each year's work, for each group of studies within the year, for each individual lesson period, and, finally, for the sections of single lessons. Each of these lesser aims should be controlled by the larger ones, and the whole should make a unified system so arranged that every piece of work done will make its contribution to the accomplishment of our final purpose.

Specimen Plans

The following plan for a Thanksgiving lesson was prepared by a teacher of seven-year-old boys and girls. The lesson came at the close of a series in-

LEARNING AND TEACHING

tended to bring to the consciousness of the pupils the fact of God's love and care:

LESSON AIM

To help pupils to see that the best way to keep Thanksgiving is to share our good things with others and to guide the sharing spirit into practical activity.

First Step

Lead the pupils in a discussion of the meaning of Thanksgiving. This will come naturally and easily, since the pupils are already thinking about Thanksgiving time.

Points to Be Emphasized

1. The historical meaning of Thanksgiving.
2. Why we celebrate Thanksgiving.

Second Step

Raise the question: "How are we going to show our Father that we are thankful?" Have the class discuss this question at some length.

Point to Be Emphasized

Merely having plenty to eat and enjoying ourselves is not enough.

Third Step

Tell the story of "Old Man Rabbit's Thanksgiving Dinner" (C. S. Bailey, *For the Story-Teller*). This story presents in a new and attractive way the familiar idea of giving Thanksgiving dinners to those in special need.

Fourth Step

Ask the question: "What do you think of old man Rabbit's plan of keeping Thanksgiving?" After a brief discussion of this question, read a letter from the Associated Charities asking for help for some needy families. Discuss this and try to develop the conclusion that the members of

THE TEACHER'S LESSON PLANS

the class can best show their gratitude by following old man Rabbit's plan and sharing their good things.

Fifth Step

Spend the remainder of the period in making definite plans for the Thanksgiving dinner.

This lesson was planned to secure results in definite Christian service. This, of course, is not the only important aim of the teacher. Other aims would demand variations of the lesson plan. The following is a plan for a lesson in "appreciation." It also was prepared for a class of seven-year-old boys and girls:

LESSON AIM

To help the pupils to an appreciation of the hymn, "We Plow the Fields," in order that they may more fully participate in the service of worship.

First Step

Previous lessons have discussed the Father's care for his children. During the last part of the last lesson period the pupils drew pictures illustrating "God's Gifts to Us." At the opening of this period have each pupil show his picture to the class and explain its meaning. These pictures will include such things as home, clothing, food, etc.

Second Step

Have a brief discussion of the pictures and say: "I am going to tell you a story of one of God's gifts." Tell the "Story of a Bag of Seeds."

Third Step

Ask the class to tell some things that the story makes them think of. They will probably tell of experiences on the farm when they saw grain growing, etc. Say to the pupils: "The story made me think of something that we have sometimes in our opening services. Can any one

169

LEARNING AND TEACHING

guess what it is?" If no one guesses, hum the air of "We Plow the Fields." If there is still no response, sing the first stanza. Some one will probably say: "Why, that tells the very same thing as our story." The teacher can suggest this in case the pupils do not.

Fourth Step

Repeat the first stanza slowly, so that the pupils can see the connection between the words of the hymn and the story of how the seed grows. Explain any words that may seem unfamiliar.

Fifth Step

"Let us all sing it together so that when it is used in the service again we may be able to sing it better with the others."

Sixth Step

After singing the stanza a couple of times ask the pupils to bow their heads and close with the following prayer: "Father, we thank thee for the seedtime and harvest, for the bright sunshine and the soft, refreshing rain."

The Relation of the Lesson to the Course

The following outlines are given to show the relation of the plan for the individual lesson to the plan for the course of which it is a part. They were prepared for use with the International Graded Lesson Course, "The Word of God in Life," prepared for students of about sixteen years of age:

PURPOSE OF THE COURSE

A brief survey of the Bible to prepare the student for later, more intensive work.

GENERAL PLAN

The rapid reading and examination of rather long sections of the Bible to get clearly the general characteristics of the various books.

170

THE TEACHER'S LESSON PLANS

PLAN FOR STUDY 40

LESSON AIM

To help the students to a realization of the practical nature of the early Hebrew laws and to enable them to make intelligent use of the books of the Pentateuch.

First Step

Discuss briefly the following questions:

1. If a woman rents a vacuum cleaner and while it is on her premises it is broken, should she or the original owner bear the expense of the repairs?

2. A little girl is attacked by a vicious dog and killed. The owner of the dog had been warned that he should keep the dog muzzled. Should the child's parents be entitled to claim damages from the owner of the dog?

3. Two men have a quarrel which ends in blows. One is badly injured. Should the other man be made to pay the hospital bill?

Second Step

Suggest that for further discussion of these questions the class be organized into a court, with one student presiding as judge and others forming the jury.

Third Step

When decisions have been rendered, compare them with the early Hebrew law. For question (1) see Exodus xxii. 14, (2) Exodus xxi. 28-31, (3) Exodus xxi. 18, 19.

Fourth Step

Close with a general discussion showing that the Ten Commandments are a statement of the fundamental principles underlying the detailed regulations.

Fifth Step

For work during the week assign to each member of the class a period of Hebrew history. Ask each one to write a brief letter or a newspaper report of the period

LEARNING AND TEACHING

as if he had been an eyewitness. Have available a list of references to supply to any student asking for help.

PLAN FOR STUDY 41

LESSON AIM

To show that the historical books of the Bible contain the story of the Hebrew people and to help the students to an understanding of the chief epochs of that history.

First Step.

Call for reports on the assignments made at the previous lesson.

Second Step

By discussion assist the student to a clear and well-organized knowledge of the periods touched upon.

Third Step

As an assignment for the following study ask each student to come prepared to read one favorite psalm and to tell in a few words what he likes about it.

These plans are quite brief and elastic. Many teachers will probably want to work out more explicit programs for the lesson periods, definitely formulating a number of the leading questions.

Underlying Principles

For the making of good lesson plans there are certain underlying conditions that must be complied with. The first is that the teacher have a clear and definite knowledeg of the pupils to be taught. Since the teacher's purpose is to change the pupils from their present manner of living to a more fully Christian plan of living, it is, of course, necessary that we understand just where the pupils are at the beginning of the lesson period. The more intimately

172

THE TEACHER'S LESSON PLANS

the teacher knows his pupils, their interests and needs, their wants and problems, the easier it is for him to plan the lesson. Recall how Jesus knew men. He went through the fields and villages, to the seashore and the hillside, wherever men lived. He feasted and he sorrowed with them; he shared the life in their homes, the temple, the market place, and the farm. None of their problems was strange to him.

Along with this knowledge of the pupils there is a question of clearness of aim. The need for this has already been emphasized. The next step is to secure a good point of contact. If we are to get their attention and interest promptly, we must begin with something about which the pupils are already thinking. The point of contact chosen should be something that can be readily developed into the central problem of the lesson. Definite thought should be given to the question of how and when new material should be introduced. There should be opportunity given for clear thinking on the part of the pupils, and provision should be made for the development of their own conclusions. Finally, the lesson plan should include provision for expression in practical living of the conclusions reached. In the Thanksgiving lesson the discussion was followed by the actual preparation of Thanksgiving dinners. In the case of the lesson on "We Plow the Fields" the practical activity consisted in singing the hymn in the class and later singing it in the service of worship. The reader will find profit in studying the sample lesson plans given above with the purpose of

173

LEARNING AND TEACHING

determining the extent to which the principles of good lesson-planning were followed in each case.

The Need for Flexibility

Sometimes objection is made to definite lesson-planning on the ground that the lesson becomes thereby stiff and mechanical and therefore both uninteresting and unfruitful. There is some justification for this objection. A plan that is too rigid may easily spoil a lesson. The teacher should not make the mistake of making an exact time-table and then following it slavishly. Things will come up in a lesson period which cannot possibly be foreseen. It will be necessary, therefore, to be always prepared for such possibilities and to adjust the prepared plan to meet the emergencies.

The fact that such adjustments are often necessary does not make it inadvisable to plan carefully in advance. It rather makes planning more urgent. It is the well-worked-out plan, not the hasty one, that can be changed and yet be workable and useful. Jesus skillfully adapted his plans to the needs of the moment. He was continually meeting with criticisms and objections, but he adjusted himself perfectly to each situation. A thorough yet flexible plan will enable the teacher to take account of unforeseen emergencies and still avoid rambling and waste and so be able to progress economically to the desired goal.

In planning for the lesson period the various elements, such as story-telling, handwork, and discussion, should not be arranged haphazard, but

THE TEACHER'S LESSON PLANS

should come in the order best suited to the accomplishment of the lesson purposes. No absolute rule can be given as to where each item should be found. In some cases the handwork may come early in the period as a review of previous work. At other times it may come as a reënforcement of the story or discussion. Care should be taken to provide sufficient variety of work to keep the lesson period from being a strain or undue tax on the pupils' power to give attention. In the case of very young children a song or some exercise involving physical activity may be introduced during the lesson period to make possible better attention for the later part of the lesson.

Learning to Plan

Ability to plan successfully may be somewhat of a native instinct, but in the main it is the result of hard work. Inexperienced teachers find it difficult to plan because they lack the knowledge that is essential to planning. Often they lack clearly defined ideas either as to the present life of the pupils, their needs and possibilities, or of the steps by which the changes sought are to be accomplished. For this reason they find planning to be difficult and also somewhat unsatisfactory. However, the very facts that make planning difficult also make it of great importance. The teacher should not cease working at the plan as long as such work seems to be making clearer and more definite the task and the method.

Teachers with more experience are liable to become weary of the labor of planning and, having acquired a certain facility in their work, to be tempt-

LEARNING AND TEACHING

ed to minimize the importance of a plan. Here is a great danger to the success of the teacher. Many teachers have labored hard to become successful and, having attained a certain standard, have remained there or gone backward. Planning should grow in both skill and profit as the teacher increases in the possession of the elements that make it possible. The need is never outgrown. Neglect of it at any stage of the work is certain to result in a falling off in effectiveness, and perhaps failure.

Questions

1. What are the essentials of a good lesson plan?
2. Select at least two lessons from the International Graded Lessons and work out teaching plans just as if you were going to teach the lessons.

176

CHAPTER XXI

TEACHING CHILDREN TO PRAY

To every Sunday-school teacher there comes the problem of teaching the pupils to pray. Whether the class consists of Beginners who have not yet learned more than a few very simple prayers, or pupils in the early teens with the enlarging social experience that comes at that time, or young people who are just finding themselves in the world of work and responsibilities, no part of the teacher's work is more important than this. At this point we enter into the holy of holies of the individual's inmost life. That many teachers hesitate to undertake the task is perhaps understandable, but the neglect of it is inexcusable. Teachers of religion should not fail to use every opportunity to bring their pupils to understand the importance of prayer and to make its values their own.

The Meaning of Prayer

Just what we will attempt to do in teaching children to pray will, of course, depend on our understanding of the meaning and use of prayer.

To begin with, we must distinguish carefully between the Christian and the non-Christian conceptions of prayer. We do not believe that prayer is a means of wheedling an unwilling God into doing something that he would really prefer not to do. It is true that sometimes people who call themselves

LEARNING AND TEACHING

Christians show some signs of this idea in their thinking and practice, but in so far as they do so they are failing to measure up to the Christian idea of prayer.

Furthermore, mere repetition of prayers is not sufficient. Buddhists have invented prayer wheels. They hold that each time the wheel revolves all of the prayers within it are offered once more to the gods to whom they are addressed. This makes of prayer a magical device. It is utterly opposed to the Christian ideal. Jesus's condemnation of the conduct of the Pharisees in this respect was unqualified: "Ye think that ye shall be heard for your much praying."

The first purpose of Christian prayer is to build up a real fellowship between God and his children. Just as friend needs and craves companionship with friend, so, and more so, do we need and reach after fellowship with the Father and Friend of all. The constant emphasis of Jesus was upon the necessity of abiding in the Father and of having the Father abide in the child.

Another purpose of prayer is to supply us with high ideals of living. We labor and play in a world that is in many respects far below the ideal. We are in constant need of a vision of things as they should be. Here prayer helps tremendously. The Christian comes from his time of prayer with new and stronger ideals. He is fired with a mighty enthusiasm to be a fellow worker with God, that his kingdom may come and his will be done. The Christian sees in God the beauty of truth and righteous-

178

TEACHING CHILDREN TO PRAY

ness, and he himself takes on something of the divine glory. He goes back to his toil with a determination that the heavenly glory shall cast its radiance over all the world.

Furthermore, prayer establishes a bond of partnership between man and God for the accomplishment of God's will. Just how and why this is so is something that the most skilled theologian cannot easily explain, but to the fact we can give abundant witness.

Learning to Pray

Since these are the fundamental purposes of Christian prayer, our task as teachers will be guided and controlled by them. We do not need to initiate the desire to pray, for the impulse is already there. It is probably quite correct to say that all men pray sometimes. Of course the form and the conditions of the prayer vary, but with all men there is at least sometimes the reaching out after help from above.

But while we recognize that prayer of some sort is a common characteristic, we also perceive that with some it is but a spasmodic and occasional practice. There is need, therefore, that we cherish and increase the desire and ability to pray.

There is also need for an enlargement of the scope of our prayer. The spirit of the oft-quoted example, "God bless me and my wife, my son John and his wife, us four and no more," is more often found than is its wording. We shrink from being so flagrantly selfish and narrow in our prayers, but we fall far short of the truly social attitude of the Master.

The teacher's task is, then, so to cherish and guide

179

LEARNING AND TEACHING

the pupil's prayer that it may be changed from an erratic impulse to an intelligent, well-directed, persistent habit of life.

Immediately there comes the question, "Can we teach prayer?" The best answer is to be found in the facts of our earlier experience. We and many others have learned to pray. Slowly there has been built up a rich experience in this highest of religious activities. Some of us have been poor pupils, but all of us have learned some things of worth. The disciples came to Jesus and asked that they be taught to pray. The request was speedily granted, and as a result the Christian Church from its earliest days has treasured the most perfect and most beautiful prayer ever composed.

How Jesus Taught Prayer

In his method of teaching prayer Jesus adopted three plans. He set his followers an example. This came first. Day after day he led with them a life which was pervaded by prayer. Then, when they came for further help, he gave them a form of prayer. Finally, he added to these some words of explanation and guidance.

In whatever order they come, these are the fundamentals in the teaching of prayer. We do not have to go far to discover the explanation of the fact that not all Church schools succeed in teaching their members to pray. We find it in the fact that real prayer is quite absent from some schools. There is perhaps no prayer in the classes, and the school and departmental assemblies are barren of real worship. The

180

TEACHING CHILDREN TO PRAY

program of the school assembly should invariably include prayer. The prayers should be such that the pupils can join in them either silently or audibly. In the school worship the pupils should not be prayed at nor prayed for, but prayed with. The leader should really *lead* the group in prayer. For the class sessions provision should be made for such privacy and freedom from interruption and distraction as will permit class and individual prayer at such times as it may seem desirable. Some classes have prayer either at the opening or at the closing of each class session.

Forms of Prayer

While fixed forms of prayer should not be used to the exclusion of other prayer, they have a place of their own and should not be neglected. They often help us to express our own faintly realized needs and cravings. We possess a considerable heritage of beautiful prayers composed by Christians both of our own and of earlier times. Some of these should be memorized and made the permanent possession of the pupils. Some classes and even schools have united to prepare special prayers for their own use. These combine something of the spontaneity of extemporaneous prayer with something of the beauty of the carefully prepared prayer.

That the prayers should be graded to the growing needs of the pupils is self-evident. The Lord's Prayer is so broadly human that it has some meaning for all kinds and conditions of people, but we need also prayers that are more specific and individual. To the extent that the prayers are pointed

181

LEARNING AND TEACHING

and localized, they become unsuitable for those who have little in common with the people by whom or for whom they were originally composed.

Of course there should be explanations of the meaning and use of prayer. Inevitably questions will arise, and the best possible answers should be given. There is no antagonism between intelligence and reverence—indeed, there is a close and vital connection. Ignorance may produce fear and dread, but knowledge and trustfulness are necessary bases for reverence and love.

Silent Prayer

A word should be said regarding the use of silent prayer. Its possibilities are very great, but in practical use it is almost always a failure. We have all known of teachers who, when their pupils failed to respond to their questions, impatiently commanded them "to think." Now, thinking is not something that can be produced on an order of this kind. Teachers are learning that good thinking is possible only on certain conditions and that if these conditions are satisfactory the pupils will be compelled to think. Instead, then, of issuing fierce commands and even threatening severe punishment, they hunt around for the faults in their work that have made impossible the kind of thinking they desire. Similarly the suggestion that we engage in silent prayer is not sufficient. When the pupils have no particular desire to pray, it is a mistake to call for silent prayer. However, when they are stirred so that their very souls clamor for utterance, then silent prayer may afford them the opportunity they need.

TEACHING CHILDREN TO PRAY

Prayer and Life

A final point of emphasis is that prayer and life cannot be separated. We say that only the good man can pray, and we also hold that prayer is essential to goodness. There is no contradiction here. The two go on together, the one helping the other. Neither righteousness nor the ability to pray is like a coat that we can put on and take off. They are rather characteristics of living that come only by growth. So we are quite right in saying that the child cannot pray till he loves, and that he cannot love unless he prays.

Questions

1. Mention some respects in which the prayer life of some boys and girls needs to be developed.

2. Thinking of a particular Sunday school or a particular class, state the steps that you would suggest as advisable in developing the prayer life of the members.

3. What are the advantages and what the disadvantages of forms of prayer?

4. Show how prayer and life are related.

CHAPTER XXII

THE EMOTIONAL LIFE OF THE LEARNER

The feelings and emotions are an element in the life of the learner that must occupy the serious attention of the teacher. The emotional life presents three problems:

1. The effective use of feeling and emotion as a motive to right living.

2. The cultivation of those permanent emotional dispositions or sentiments that give added value, richness, and significance to life.

3. The control of hurtful and unworthy emotions and the guarding against emotional excesses and fruitless sentimentalism.

Feeling as a Motive

The elementary and fundamental feeling qualities are agreeableness and disagreeableness, or satisfaction and discomfort. The rôle of these elementary forms of feeling in the learning process has been emphasized already in earlier chapters. The law of effect, which we have recognized as one of the fundamental laws of learning, indicates that the agreeableness or disagreeableness of an action is a potent factor in determining whether or not that action shall become a permanent element in the life of the learner. Those modes of conduct whose consequences are satisfying will tend to be repeated; those whose consequences produce discomfort will tend to be avoided.

THE EMOTIONAL LIFE OF THE LEARNER

Actions that are in line with the interests and desires of the learner will be satisfying; others will not. Interest in the activity itself or in the ends to which it naturally leads is the most effective motive in learning, because the doing of interesting things is accompanied by a glow of satisfaction.

We may, then, recognize the fact that it is really the feeling aspect of life that gives it value, significance, worth. Whether life be worth living or not depends upon the feelings that accompany life's experiences.

The way in which things *affect* us—in other words, the emotional reactions that they arouse—is what determines their worth for us and our conduct with reference to them. Man does not live in a bare, drab, neutral world of intellectual facts and mechanical motor activities. The knowledge that controls conduct is that which arouses feeling, which stirs the emotions. It is not knowledge of threatening danger that makes the volunteer soldier; it is the patriotic thrill that accompanies the knowledge. It is not knowledge of conditions in the slums or in foreign lands that makes missionaries; it is the fervor of sympathy that accompanies this knowledge. Only in doing something to alleviate these conditions can the sympathetic impulse find satisfaction. A mastery of the science of government or of the facts of the nation's history is ineffective in making good citizens unless there be stirred in the student the feeling of patriotism and loyalty. Knowledge of creeds and dogmas and theological doctrines, knowledge of the Bible as literature, or of the facts of

185

LEARNING AND TEACHING

Church history, is no substitute for the emotions of love and reverence and awe felt in the presence of God the Father. When these emotions become genuine elements of the learner's experience, his life will be controlled by them inevitably, where bare intellectual conviction and comprehension might utterly fail to influence conduct.

Whatever the considerations that govern conduct, it is the potency of the feeling accompanying these considerations that gives them determinative force. Even when it is so abstract a thing as love of truth, this *love* is a feeling. Facts and truth unaccompanied by feeling would lose their power to control conduct.

We must, then, as teachers not be content with merely giving our pupils facts or with conducting them mechanically through certain kinds of action. We must see to it that the facts awaken genuine feeling, so that they may influence life. We must cultivate right feelings in our pupils, because feeling determines conduct.

Cultivating the Feelings

It is this potency in determining ways of living that gives the feelings their importance for the teacher. This is true even of those emotional dispositions, complex and permanently established in the life, that we call sentiments. These are worthy when they impel to worthy living, unworthy when their outcome is unworthy. But because they are related to life as a whole rather than to specific experiences, and because they play so large a part in

186

THE EMOTIONAL LIFE OF THE LEARNER

life, we think of certain sentiments as worthy of cultivation for their own sake, because of the added richness and value and significance they give to life. Horne quotes Dr. Eliot as saying: "The sentiments which American schools ought to cherish and inculcate are family love, respect for law and public order, love of freedom, and reverence for truth and righteousness." Hartshorne writes, in his "Worship in the Sunday School": "The Christian attitudes suitable to children from the first to the eighth grades (and, indeed, when properly defined, for other ages as well) might be summed up under the rubrics Gratitude, Good Will, Reverence, Faith, and Loyalty." These are given merely as a sample list of sentiments that the teacher should try to cultivate.

We must cultivate right feelings, emotions, and sentiments. But how? The cultivation of the emotional life must be in the main indirect. We must remember, in the first place, that it is not a question of *creating* emotions, but of *arousing* and *cultivating* them. The emotions and the instincts are closely related. The emotional life has an instinctive basis —that is to say, certain kinds of objects naturally call forth the emotions of love, anger, fear, joy, and so on. These tendencies are instinctive or inherited. They are a feature of original human nature. But various things have the power to call forth these instinctive reactions. Which things shall permanently retain their power depends upon which things are first and most often responded to. This means, for example, that what the individual comes to love

187

LEARNING AND TEACHING

with an abiding love or to hate with an abiding hate will be those things that have *first* and *most often* called forth love or hate. The practical application of this principle is obvious. The way to control the emotional life is to control experience in general. The emotions cannot be isolated from other aspects of mental life. If we would have our pupils love good and true and beautiful things, we must keep them in the presence of the good and the true and the beautiful. If we would have them abhor evil, we must see to it that vice is shown to be repulsive. The danger in much of modern popular fiction is that vice and sin are presented in alluring disguises and falsely cloaked in the garments of beauty and virtue. Such insidiousness is much more to be dreaded than the coarse obscenity of some of our earlier English novelists.

The emotional life is to be cultivated, then, by seeing to the atmosphere in which the learner lives, seeing to it that the right things are allowed to stimulate the emotions. When they have done this often enough, wrong things will no longer have power. When right things have been presented and given their chance, little is to be accomplished by talking about the emotions that ought to be felt. The objects and experiences must be trusted to make their own appeal. If they do not, we may find the explanation either in some previous experiences where wrong emotional associations have been established or in the fact that the proper maturity for that particular emotional response has not been attained. At any rate, urging cannot create the emotion that

188

THE EMOTIONAL LIFE OF THE LEARNER

does not occur spontaneously. It may call forth a pretense of it, but nothing can be more reprehensible and dangerous to sincerity of feeling and integrity of character than pretending to feel emotions that are not really felt. Sincerity in the emotional life, whether moral, æsthetic, or religious, is certainly the first requisite. We must trust worthy things to call forth desirable responses. We may be sure that the individual who has experienced only the true, the beautiful, and the good will respond to them only with love, joy, and reverence.

The Influence of the Surroundings

It is in the general atmosphere of the Sunday school and in the service of worship and praise that the feeling life is the primary concern. The general principle that should govern here has just been suggested: keep the pupil in the presence of the best. Real music and genuine religious thought and feeling that are within the child's comprehension should characterize the songs instead of ragtime and doggerel. Beautiful pictures and tasteful, cheery surroundings; services of prayer and worship that express attitudes and ideals that the child is capable of understanding and entering into, carried out in a spirit of genuine reverence, but free from cant or mock solemnity—these are some of the agencies that the Sunday school may use in cultivating the emotional life of its pupils. Detailed suggestions are out of place here. But this may be urged: too much care and attention cannot be given to these features of the Sunday school. We are falling short of our oppor-

LEARNING AND TEACHING

tunity when "any old room" will do for the Sunday-school class; when our songs and our prayers are merely "opening exercises," at most perfunctory, confused, trivial, and in many schools valued according to the noise and enthusiasm alone; when our songs are ugly, shallow, vapid, even immoral and irreligious, silly in wording and thought and "raggy" in tune. There is no chance to develop fine feeling through such means.

The pupils will probably not be reverent and earnest if the officers and teachers are quite the reverse. Feeling is contagious. The teacher cannot hope to call forth in his pupils an emotional response that he himself is incapable of. To show the desired feeling is a most effective way of eliciting it. To pretend to feelings not really experienced is, of course, fatal to influence. The child quickly detects sham and insincerity. But genuine appreciation of the beautiful, respect for righteousness and truth and sincerity, love for God, sympathy for and interest in others, manifested simply and sincerely, will inevitably produce their like. Nothing is more potent as an educative force than personality, the power of example.

Developing Right Feelings

Control of the emotions is indirect, we have said. And this leads to some practical suggestions that are especially valuable for the learner himself to know and adopt. The first is this: One of the best ways to arouse an emotion is to "go through the motions." This is not to urge pretense. It sim-

THE EMOTIONAL LIFE OF THE LEARNER

ply means using legitimate means to cultivate right feelings and get rid of wrong ones. Acting in the line of the emotions one ought to have is an effective way of inducing the emotions. "At a given time," says Henry Churchill King, "a man may be feeling far from cheerful and without courage. This at least he can do: he can take a good, long breath and stiffen up his backbone and put on the mien of cheer and courage; and in so doing he is far more apt to become cheerful and courageous. . . . It is to no man's credit to act as illy as he feels. He is rather bound often to act much better than he feels. And so acting, he will be helped to better feeling."

Avoiding Unworthy Emotions

The second suggestion relates to the control and avoidance of unworthy emotions. The only way to keep an object or an idea from arousing the emotional attitude associated with it is to get it out of consciousness. Get away from the thing or get busy thinking of something else. "The small boy who is looking through a fence at a patch of watermelons that is not his cannot prevent his mouth from watering; *but he can run.*" It is useless to continue to think of the thing that is arousing evil feelings and impulses, saying all the time, "I won't feel"; "I won't do the wrong thing"; or even saying, "I won't think of it any more." The only way to avoid the wrong feelings and impulses is to quit thinking of the thing, and the only way to quit thinking of the thing is to think of something else. The only way to get rid of an idea is to put some other idea in

191

LEARNING AND TEACHING

its place. That is, too, the only way to keep an idea from controlling action. And the richer the store of fine ideas, noble memories, and associations with fine ideas and inspiring personalities one has, the more surely can he displace the evil thought with a good one. "Be not overcome of evil, but overcome evil with good" is sound psychology. The best resource in such times of temptation is the ability to turn to Jesus. And this ability can come only through having been persistently in his presence. In continued association with him is the surest escape from sinful feelings and sinful deeds.

Self-Control

We need to consider, finally, certain dangers in the emotional life that need to be carefully guarded against. In the first place, it is well to recognize the fact that intense emotional disturbance interferes with clear thought and efficient action. The baseball player whose practice stops and throws are perfect may at a critical moment in the game throw the ball over the first baseman's head. The excitement has robbed him of the ability to control his actions. It is the man who keeps his head, who keeps cool, who resists the impulse to emotional excitement that saves lives and property in a fire or a railroad wreck. It is he alone who can think and act efficiently.

This fact has significance in the religious life. It is not in the periods of intense emotional disturbance that character is built. Such experiences are often effective in breaking down old habits, in clearing the

THE EMOTIONAL LIFE OF THE LEARNER

ground for the formation of new and better ones, in leading to new points of view and resolutions for better living. But such upheavals are only a means to an end. Considered in and for itself, the excitement is a "disorganizing experience; but if from this travail of the soul there be born a better life, then the emotion has value." And this end of better living may not always require this kind of emotional crisis. Neither insisting upon one particular type of experience nor making the emotion an end in itself can be justified. After all, it is the result, not the process, that matters. We quote Henry Churchill King again: "Religion, like any ideal view, is never primarily interested in the mechanism of the process, whether gradual or sudden, but in the significance of the process. Its question is never, How did the thing come to be? but, What does it mean? What is its end? The change itself is the vital and significant thing; *it* must be the witness of the divineness of the work." The Scriptural teaching is: "By their fruits ye shall know them." And "the fruit of the Spirit is love, joy, peace, long-suffering, kindness, goodness, faithfulness, meekness, self-control." We need to guard against hysterical loss of self-control. There can be no surrender of self in the absence of self-possession and self-direction.

Emotion and Action

And, further, we need to guard against emotions, however commendable, that do not lead to action. Mere excitement that leads nowhere is dissipation, whether religious or moral or some other kind.

LEARNING AND TEACHING

James has eloquently expressed the danger here: "A tendency to act only becomes effectively ingrained in us in proportion to the uninterrupted frequency with which the actions actually occur, and the brain 'grows' to their use. When a resolve or a fine glow of feeling is allowed to evaporate without bearing practical fruit, it is worse than a chance lost; it works so as positively to hinder future resolutions and emotions from taking the normal path of discharge. There is no more contemptible type of human character than that of the nerveless sentimentalist and dreamer who spends his life in a weltering sea of sensibility and emotion, but who never does a manly concrete deed."[1]

All this means that those emotional experiences that are really valuable and potent forces in life are those that are preceded and followed by constant effort to form Christian ideals and standards, to develop the habit of persistent association with Christ, and to train in Christian service and Christian living.

Questions

1. Point out the importance of the emotions in the education of the individual.

2. What are some of the ways in which the emotions may be cultivated?

3. What is the best method of controlling undesirable emotions?

4. Why is it necessary to see that emotions issue in action?

---

[1]"Psychology," pages 147, 148.

CHAPTER XXIII

THE TEACHER'S FELLOW WORKERS

IN the realization that as teachers we are not working alone, but are coöperating with a group of educators, there is both a challenge and an inspiration. We are called to more thorough devotion to our work by the knowledge that what we do is part of a larger whole and that on our efforts depends in a measure the success of the whole undertaking. We are encouraged by knowing that our work is strengthened and magnified by the coöperation of our fellow laborers. That we may coöperate most effectively with them we must spend some time in a study of the wider relationships of the teacher's work.

The School

The teacher's most immediate contact with the larger educational group is through the school itself. The pupils of the class have brought with them the training of their earlier years in the school and are now preparing for work in more advanced classes. More than that, every session brings together a group many times larger than that of the class, and this is educationally important. We have all had evidence of the fact that a single disorderly class lowers the morale of the whole school. It is not so evident, but none the less true, that high standards in one part of the school have an elevating influence on the other sections. There flow from individual

195

LEARNING AND TEACHING

to individual and from group to group ideas, and especially attitudes, that, for good or for ill, have important educational effects.

The educational importance of the larger group is perhaps not sufficiently recognized and used. What we are accustomed to call "teaching" is carried on best in the closely graded class, but there are certain other educational results well worth attaining for which the class work is inadequate. The departmental session has an indispensable share in the religious education of our pupils. Worship is something that requires in the main a larger group than that of the class. Similarly, the educational values to be obtained from the social activities of our pupils call for units that are larger than class groups.

There is also the matter of school spirit. This is well worth cultivating, for it is a powerful controlling force in the making of character. The old method of having the whole school assemble once or twice during each session was based on wrong educational propositions and, fortunately, is rapidly disappearing. It did, however, have some value as a means of unifying the school, and this aspect of the matter is well worth preserving. For this purpose school picnics and school social evenings have real value. There is a decided advantage in occasional assemblies of the whole school, but at such times care should be taken to prepare a program that will be appreciated by the whole school and will therefore accomplish its real purpose. The great festive occasions—Christmas, Easter, and Thanksgiving—lend

THE TEACHER'S FELLOW WORKERS

themselves especially to the cultivation of these larger social relationships.

Another important method of securing unity is through the adoption of certain larger missionary and other service projects. Each class should have its special interest, but some things should be taken up by the departments, and the entire school should occasionally undertake some common task. At the dedication of a fine, new building for religious education completed a few weeks before the writing of these paragraphs each class in the school pledged itself to a certain sum to be contributed weekly for the period of five years. The amount of money secured in this way will be large, but more important than the amount will be the educational result. That school will experience a unity of spirit and purpose that will be of inestimable value.

The Church

But not only are the teachers and the pupils members of a school; they are members of a Church. We are coming to realize again what we had for a time almost forgotten, that the whole Church is or should be primarily an educational institution. Its business is not so much that of teaching how to settle a quarrel as of developing the kind of life that does not quarrel. It seeks not so much to relieve suffering and sorrow as to teach men how to prevent them. Its business is not so much to supply amusement as to show us how to enjoy the really great things in life. Its great aim and purpose is not to dispense salvation, but to lead us into the knowledge and love of

LEARNING AND TEACHING

God, in whom alone there is eternal life. This is the institution of which the school forms a part. The teacher's work is a contribution to its main purpose, and it in turn places at the teacher's disposal its strength and resources. Occasionally a school develops such an exalted idea of its own importance that it overshadows the church of which it is a part. The disastrous consequences of such a situation are second only to those experienced when the church forgets that it has an educational task.

For the development of a spirit of loyalty to the larger group included in the local church there should be careful planning and effort. Teachers and pupils should be led to feel that the school is neither apart from nor alongside of the church, but is a part of the church—is, in fact, the church carrying on its educational work.

The Family

Within recent years we have had a new emphasis on the educational importance of the family. With the development of numerous community and state institutions, some had come to the point of saying that the importance of the family was diminishing. More careful thought, however, speedily revealed the error of such a conclusion. The prolonged and intimate social contacts of family life with the mighty power of family loyalty and love make the family the most powerful educational institution in existence. What the family does for the development of character can never be wholly undone, and what it fails to do can never be entirely made up. The

THE TEACHER'S FELLOW WORKERS

teacher who expects to have any real success must take into account the work of the family and must coöperate with it. The church school can perform no higher duty than that of helping the parents to be real religious educators.

The State School

We often hear the ill-founded charge that our public school system is Godless and irreligious. It is true that the school does not do or undertake to do all that should be done for the moral and religious development of our young people, but its contribution is nevertheless extensive and important. Our best educational leaders continually declare that the ultimate aim of the state school is a moral one; that mere knowledge of science, of industry, of trade, and of literature takes on real value only when it is controlled by purposes that are for the welfare of mankind.

But, besides this harmony of purpose, we look to the state school to supply us many of the prerequisites to religious education. Our work in the church school is greatly facilitated by the ability on the part of the pupils to read and write, to think and appreciate. Without these we would be greatly hampered and delayed. We need, therefore, a better understanding of the mutual relationships of the state school and the school for religious education.

We need to realize that each contributes to the other's purpose and that only by community of effort and division of labor can we accomplish our aims. Every Sunday-school teacher whose pupils

199

LEARNING AND TEACHING

are school attendants should make it his business to know as much as he can of the day school life of the members of his class.

The Community

Our day has witnessed an enlarged emphasis on the importance of community life, but it will probably take long hammering on the topic before we really wake up to its importance. From our discussion of "Learning from Our Associates" it should be easily evident that we cannot have a clean individual in a dirty community and that we cannot raise the standards of living of one person without thereby elevating somewhat the life of the community in which he dwells. We cannot say which is first in our educational work, for the two must go together; but we can say that neither can make satisfactory progress if the other lags seriously behind. The community is to the teacher of religion both a challenge and an asset. It calls for an interest and an effort on behalf of more than the class of which he is teacher, and it assures him the coöperative effort of others of like ideals and purposes.

Literature

Within the last few years there has been made available to religious teachers a greatly enlarged amount and variety of literature prepared especially for their work. Indeed, providing its workers with an educational reference library is considered to be an essential mark of the successful church school. The teacher who does not draw on the resources of

200

THE TEACHER'S FELLOW WORKERS

educational literature is seriously handicapping himself in his work.

In the matter of adequate literature for the pupils our educational consciousness is scarcely so well awake as in the provision of material for teachers. Unfortunately, there are still schools which in purchasing lesson helps pay more attention to the price than to the quality. The utmost care should be used in the purchase of pupils' helps to see that not only the paper, type, and illustrations are of at least equal quality with that found in the textbooks of the secular schools, but that the content is the best obtainable.

Questions

1. Show how the whole school works with the teacher for the attainment of our purposes.

2. Mention some methods by which "school spirit" may be developed.

3. What is the real relationship of the school and the church?

4. Of how much importance to our religious educational program is the Christian family?

5. In what ways may the state school and the Sunday school coöperate for common purposes?

6. Show how a high type of community life is an advantage to the boys and girls.

CHAPTER XXIV

EVANGELISM THROUGH TEACHING

We are constantly being reminded that evangelism is the chief concern of the church. We are told—and we heartily concur in the statement—that the real task of the church school is evangelism; that we as religious educators should measure our work first of all by that standard.

Two Aspects of the Problem

Even a hasty examination of the topic of evangelism will reveal the fact that there are two main aspects of the matter, the human and the divine. That evangelism is not entirely within the control of human thought and effort is so well known that debate on the point is unreasonable. The transformation of life always demands more than human power. We can simply say: "It is His doing, and it is wonderful in our eyes."

But that there is a human side to evangelism is also very evident. Since the beginning of Christian history we have had numerous examples of men and women and boys and girls led to the Master through the ministry of preachers and teachers. Sermons and personal conversations have been followed by such changes in the living of certain people that we are compelled to believe their testimony when they say that they have experienced the presence of God in their lives.

EVANGELISM THROUGH TEACHING

What, then, are the conditions of successful evangelism? Is it true that some are susceptible to a religious appeal and that others are not? Or is it a difference in time or mood? Or are there such definite principles and rules in the matter that by careful study we can find guidance for our work? The importance of the topic suggests that we should do our utmost to discover ways of making our preaching and teaching and personal conversation effective in the accomplishment of the purpose that we hold to be supreme.

The Main Elements

In the work of the evangelist we discover three main elements. His work assumes the knowledge of the will of God. The evangelist finds the largest response to his appeal among those whose early lives have been spent in Christian homes and Christian communities. With these people it is a case of failing to live up to their own ideals. They know better than they do, and they need the sting of conscience to call them to better living. When the evangelist approaches those who know little of the meaning of Christianity, his first task is to declare unto them the will of God.

The second step in conversion is the adoption of the Christian ideal as one's own, the acceptance of Christ and his way of life. Without this the most thorough knowledge of the truth is of little value. There must be choice; there must be decision. To the knowledge of God's will must be added a stern determination to do his will.

The third step in the process is the continued reg-

LEARNING AND TEACHING

ulation of life in accordance with the Christian ideal, the establishment of the habit of Christian living. Conversion is not a thing of a minute, but of a whole life. It is not an experience which comes and goes away, but which remains, and because of which the life afterwards is never what it was before. So conversion in the larger sense is not merely the exhilarating experience of a moment, but the transformation of the whole of life into the likeness of Christ Jesus.

Evangelistic Teaching

Looked at in this way, it becomes evident that teaching is not something over against evangelism, but is a part of the evangelical process. Sometimes teaching has been regarded as distinct from evangelism because the words were too narrowly defined. Teaching is often thought of merely as the process of imparting information or of compelling the pupils to memorize something. This is far from an adequate definition. The real teacher is one who helps to build life. As religious educators our work fails unless our pupils not only possess information about Christ and the Christian religion, but accept him and his standards as their own and regulate their lives accordingly.

Another reason why evangelism and teaching have been considered as distinct has been due to a narrow interpretation of the meaning of evangelism. We sometimes lay the emphasis, either entirely or chiefly, on the *decision* to accept Christ. This is really only one of three steps in evangelism. It should be evident how empty and worthless the decision must

204

EVANGELISM THROUGH TEACHING

be unless there be also a knowledge of the meaning of the Christian life and the establishment of habits in harmony with that knowledge.

Practical Suggestions

A few practical suggestions that have grown out of experience in educational evangelism may be helpful. We should not forget that at about twelve years of age and again at about sixteen there comes to most young people a peculiar sensitiveness to a religious appeal. It is, of course, very important that our young people should not pass these sensitive periods without feeling the call of Christ, but this does not mean that the evangelistic aim should be confined to these times. Sensitivity to the Christian appeal is never wholly absent, and at no time should we do anything that would close the door to our young people.

Decision Day has been an effective evangelistic occasion in our Sunday schools; but in the light of what has just been said, it will readily appear that the opportunity to definitely accept Christ as a personal Saviour should not be confined to any day or date. It is not for teacher or superintendent to say when their pupils should give themselves to Christ. The way is always open. Their development in this respect should be neither forced nor retarded. There is great danger lest in waiting for Decision Day we let slip the real climax in the pupil's own experience. There is also danger of securing a decision without adequate preparation and thus robbing the pupil of a very rich experience. It is commonly agreed that

LEARNING AND TEACHING

a Decision Day that is unprepared for cannot possibly be successful and may easily do more harm than good.

It is particularly important that we make allowance for differences amongst our pupils. The fact that some pupils are more demonstrative and make their feelings more evident than others does not necessarily mean that their experience is more real and vital. The very opposite may be the case. The real test lies, not in the intensity of the emotional disturbance, but in the degree to which life becomes really Christian.

In the effort to lead the pupils to a definite decision good teaching demands that the emphasis should be positive rather than negative. Instead of asking them to give up, we should invite them to do something they have not done before and let the good crowd out the evil. Being a Christian means giving up some things, of course; but it involves less of giving up than of obtaining. The teacher should emphasize this positive side of the experience.

The Vision of the Future

From what has been said in the preceding chapters, it will be evident that the work of the Sunday-school teacher offers a splendid opportunity for Christian service. It challenges the very best that is in us. The task demands not only real ability, but hard study and patient work; but the results to be accomplished are worth all the effort required.

Looking into the future, we feel that there is much uncertainty as to the changes that will shortly

EVANGELISM THROUGH TEACHING

take place in the social life of the world. Of one thing, however, there is no uncertainty—there will be an increased need for the moral control of life, for the spirit of Christ in daily living. The moral problems in the days ahead will be not unlike those we have faced before. We owe it to our nation, we owe it to the family of nations, we owe it to our Master, and we owe it to our boys and girls to make the best possible preparation for Christian leadership.

Questions

1. Point out some aspects of evangelism that are quite beyond human control.

2. Show how human beings can be "fellow laborers with God" for the evangelizing of the world.

3. What are the main elements of evangelism?

4. How are evangelism and religious education related?

5. Why is it that religious education and evangelism have sometimes been considered as different?

6. What reasons have you for holding that teaching in the Sunday school is a Christian service of the highest importance?

2- 8681

BV Sheridan
1533 Learning & Teaching
S55
570012
Delos James
6050 Woodlawn

2- 8681

CPSIA information can be obtained
at www.ICGtesting.com
Printed in the USA
BVHW030058200722
642495BV00004B/120